BYRON

A Poet Dangerous to Know

BYRON
A Poet Dangerous to Know

———————————— ❧❧ ————————————

by GEOFFREY TREASE

"Bad, mad and dangerous to know."
—*Lady Caroline Lamb (of Byron)*

———————————— ❧❧ ————————————

HOLT, RINEHART AND WINSTON
New York   Chicago   San Francisco

Author's Note

In 1968 permission was granted, after several refusals in earlier years, to erect a tablet to Byron in Westminster Abbey, where, nearly a century and a half before, his body had been denied burial among the nation's other famous men.

At last it seems that the prejudice against him has lost its power. Generations of boys and girls at school, while expected to study and appreciate his poems, have been discouraged from asking awkward questions about his life. Byron was not approved of, not an example to set before the young.

This attitude is no longer acceptable. Byron had many faults, and was the first to admit them. Yet it is arguable that he caused less unhappiness to innocent people than did the well-meaning and idealistic Shelley, whom it is permissible to admire.

In any case, admiration is not the first concern of an honest biographer.

To tell Byron's story attracted me because he seems to have been a person with whom modern young people should find a special sympathy. He too was in revolt against his elders, against convention, against repressive government, whether at home or abroad. He was wild, witty, and outrageous. He was kind and cruel by turns, mean and generous, brilliantly imaginative and unforgivably thoughtless—a young man, in short, not to be set upon a pedestal, but one who, with his bubbling high spirits and shocking opinions, would be the life and soul of many a group today.

Because he loved to shock, he often said things he did not mean. This has to be allowed for when writing, and reading, his story. But at least it is possible, thanks to the preservation of his own letters and his friends', and of countless jottings, journals, and reminiscences of those who knew him, to piece together most of that story in great detail. In this book, for instance, every line of quoted dialogue is taken from the records, and Byron's own thoughts and feelings are indicated only as he himself set them down.

G. T.

Contents

Illustrations follow page 86

EDGAR HOLLOWAY

RUSSIA

POLAND

RUSSIA

Byron's tour, 1809–1811
Byron's journey, 1816
Byron's last journey, 1823

0   100   200   300
MILES

R. Danube

VIENNA

BUDAPEST

AUSTRIAN EMPIRE

Carpathians

BUCHAREST

BELGRADE

BLACK SEA

Verona

Venice

Ravenna

eghorn

ROME

Naples

I T A L Y

OTTOMAN

Hellespont

Constantinople

ALBANIA

Jannina

G R E E C E

Missolonghi

AEGEAN SEA

Troy

EMPIRE

TURKEY

Ithaca

Cephalonia

Delphi

Marathon

Smyrna

Ephesus

SICILY

Strait of Messina

Gulf of Corinth

ATHENS

Rhodes

MALTA

CRETE

A N   S E A

❧ 1 ❧

"A Boy at Aberdeen"

THEY must, the boy knew, be very near. These ragged belts of woodland, oaks bent like old men under masses of August greenery, were remnants of Sherwood Forest. Milestones had begun to mention "Nottingham."

There had been so many milestones, tollhouses, turnpikes, posting inns to change horses and snatch food and sleep. Nearly four hundred miles they had driven, up hill and down dale, from northeast Scotland to the English Midlands.

The coach halted. Yet another tollhouse! An old woman stepped forward for the money. This, then, was Newstead. His mother poked her head out. He was conscious of the false note in her voice as she asked the question to which she already knew the answer:

"Who lives on this estate?"

"It was Lord Byron's, ma'am, but he is dead."

His mother pressed the question. "And who is the heir now?"

"They say," replied the old woman, "it's a little boy that lives at Aberdeen."

What his mother would have said next he was never to know. The drama of the moment was too much for their servant, May.

"This is him, God bless him!" she burst out. And seizing the embarrassed boy, she gave him a noisy kiss.

The turnpike let them through, the coach rolled on, and George Gordon, sixth Lord Byron, entered into his ancient heritage.

The boy, for all his broad Scots speech at that time, had been born in London.

The house, at 16 Holles Street, was demolished about a hundred years later, although by then Byron's fame had earned a medallion on its wall, identifying it as his birthplace. In any case, the building would not have survived the Second World War, when the whole street was destroyed by bombs. Today the exact spot where the poet came into the world is untraceable.

Byron would probably be glad that his birthplace has vanished so completely and that pilgrims cannot go to stare at it.

He was fiercely proud and he would have taken no pleasure in remembering the circumstances of those early days.

As he learned, when he was old enough to understand such things, the humble house in the London side street had not even been his home. His mother had merely rented a room there while awaiting the birth of her child. The place was cheap but respectable enough. Mrs. Byron was a lady of good Scottish ancestry, and although she had inherited money, now she had very little left.

That was the fault of her husband, Captain John Byron, who had earned the nickname of Mad Jack by his completely immoral and scoundrelly behavior. He had been married before, stealing another man's wife to make her his own after the necessary divorce—and divorce itself was a rare thing in the eighteenth century, seldom obtained except by wealthy aristocrats. When she died, hastened to her grave by his heartless treatment, Mad Jack lost no time in marrying again, not for love but for money.

This second wife, to be the mother of the poet, was Catherine Gordon, an ignorant, plain, and rather stupid young woman, with two advantages from Captain Byron's point of view: she had inherited estates in Aberdeenshire and she was a solitary orphan, brought up by a grandmother as ignorant as herself, and so an easy victim for a fortune hunter with his swaggering charm. Within a year or two he had run through as much of her money as he could lay hands on. They moved from Scotland to France, leaving debts behind them wherever they went. Late in 1787 Mrs. Byron crossed to England, so that their child could be born in London. The Captain did not follow her until January of the new year, and even then he did not share the lodgings in Holles Street.

There was a good reason for that. In 1788, and for long afterwards, right into the period depicted by Charles Dickens, the English law had a rough way with debtors. If Mad Jack had shown his face in London, he would have been seized by his creditors and thrown into jail, to rot there indefinitely until somehow his debts were paid. On Sundays, however, he was safe. A debtor could not be arrested on the Sabbath. So, slipping quietly across the Channel from France, he went into hiding in a convenient place outside London, where no one could track him down. On Sundays he emerged from hiding, visited his wife, and disappeared again.

These were the unpromising circumstances—they can hardly be described as a "home" or a "family"—into which George Gordon Byron was born on Tuesday, January 22, 1788.

To add to his misfortunes, he was born with a clubfoot. His right foot was twisted sideways, and he was fated to limp through life.

It is unlikely that Captain Byron ventured to attend his son's christening at Marylebone Church a few weeks later. Probably the two godfathers were not there either. One was the Duke of Gordon, whom Mrs. Byron could claim as a kinsman without much difficulty, for the ancient Gordon family had 157 traceable branches. In choosing the baby's names, however, she was commemorating her own dead father, George Gordon. Mrs. Byron might have lost most of her money, but she kept her passionate family pride. She never forgot that she had royal Stuart blood, being descended from the poet king, James I of Scotland. Nor was her son allowed to grow up without that knowledge.

The Byrons could not boast royal blood, but they belonged to the nobility, and this was an age when nobility was of first importance, though it was embarrassing when there was no money to back it.

The date, 1788, is worth noting. It was the year before the fall of the Bastille and the rise of the common people against the aristocrats of France. It was a mere twelve years since the Declaration of Independence. In Britain and in Europe, few had yet grasped the significance of the United States or the new concept that all men were born equal. Byron can be understood, as a person, only if he is seen clearly against the background of the world into which he was born, and in which he lived his whole short, tempestuous life—a world in which title mattered more than talent and a man was respected not for the poetry he wrote but for the peerage he inherited.

The Byrons had been knights in the Middle Ages. In 1540, when Henry VIII closed down all the English monasteries, he had granted to the family the priory of Newstead in Sherwood Forest, and in due time this home had become known, not quite accurately, as Newstead Abbey. In the Civil War the Byrons had served King Charles I: it is said that there had been seven of them fighting on the Cavalier side at the Battle of Edgehill. As a reward for his services, Sir John Byron had been made Lord Byron. Strictly speaking, he became a baron, which put him on the lowest rung of the ladder in the English peerage, there being five such rungs, with dukes at the top, then marquises, earls, and viscounts. But all, even the barons, had equal privileges: to vote in the House of Lords (for "peer" means "equal") and to hand on their titles to their eldest sons or the member of the family next in line.

By 1788 the barony was held by the fifth Lord Byron, the uncle of Mad Jack, himself known as the Wicked Lord.

Wild stories were told of him. Of some there was no doubt: he had quarreled with one of his Nottinghamshire neighbors, William Chaworth, after dinner in a London tavern, fought a duel with swords in a candlelit room, and killed his opponent. Charged with murder, he had been sent to the Tower of London and put on trial by the House of Lords. Such were the privileges of a nobleman that he was not to be lodged in a common prison, and was to be tried literally by his peers, men of the same status as himself. Lord Byron was acquitted of murder but found guilty of manslaughter. He was quickly set free and retired to Newstead, where he became an eccentric recluse. The gay London life he had formerly loved was now barred to him. If he had to visit the city on business, he went quietly under another name.

He had had three sons. Two died young. The survivor refused to marry the heiress chosen for him and eloped with his own cousin. After that, the Wicked Lord shut himself off even from his own family. His wife left him: it was said, probably untruthfully, that he had thrown her into the lake. He carried pistols everywhere, and had them laid on his dining table along with the knives and forks. In his bedroom he always kept the sword with which he had killed William Chaworth. Apart from a favored servant nicknamed Lady Betty, the only living creatures in which he showed much interest were the crickets that he was said to have tamed and taught to hop about on him.

Mrs. Byron knew how useless it would be to appeal for help to the head of her husband's family. She had indeed, and with good reason, a poor opinion of the Byrons as a tribe. When, as her child grew up, she would lose her temper with him and fly into one of her rages, she would shout at him: "You little dog! You're a Byron all over—you're as bad as your father!"

Mad Jack and the Wicked Lord were in fact only conspicuous examples of a family famous for uncontrollable behavior. Their Latin motto, *Crede Biron* (Trust Byron), was ironical. Few of the Byrons could be trusted to do anything except act like Byrons.

If Mrs. Byron had known more of her own family history, she would have realized that the Gordons also had a bloodstained record of violence and banditry down the centuries.

In short, her child came into the world not only with the handicaps of a clubfoot, poverty, and parents continually at loggerheads, but also with a heredity on both sides that promised nothing but trouble.

A child cannot remember the first year of its life, and no one else has kept a record of Mrs. Byron's movements after she left Holles Street. That is understandable, for she and her husband had every reason to avoid notice. He owed thirteen hundred pounds—and if someone had been foolish enough to pay his debts for him, the Captain would at once have run up more. A gentleman of quality, as the phrase then ran, was not expected to earn his living by working at a profession, still less at a trade. He was supposed to live on the rents of land and property he owned, or the interest from investments, or from money inherited by the woman he had married. Failing an income from such sources, he could only borrow—and not repay.

Mrs. Byron's inheritance had by now dwindled to a few thousand pounds. A wife in those days had no control over her own money. It went straight into the hands of her husband. The only way to save it from a husband like Mad

Jack was to set up a trust, whereby the trustees, honest and reliable people, could keep tight hold of the capital and pay out only the interest to the wife.

By this method Mrs. Byron was able to draw an income of one hundred and fifty pounds a year, enough for her and the baby to live on, but useless to a man of Mad Jack's spendthrift habits. The several thousand pounds of capital, which he would have squandered in no time, were kept safe. He could not touch them, but neither could she.

Sometime in 1789 Mrs. Byron went back to her native Scotland and took an apartment in Queen Street, Aberdeen, an ancient port on the east coast, known as the granite city and also as the silver city by the sea, because of the way the fine stone buildings sparkled in the clear light reflected from those cold northern waters.

This was the boy's world until he was ten: the harbor with its fishing boats, proud sailing ships, and circling gulls; the two rivers, Dee and Don, rushing to the sea; the cathedral and the grammar school; the market place, the streets of elegant eighteenth-century houses mingled with the gabled, small-windowed dwellings of an earlier age. He grew up in those streets and in the countryside bordering the town, and he never forgot them. "In my memory as yesterday," he once declared, was the "brig" over the River Don, "with its one arch, and its black deep salmon stream below." His love of mountains was born during a holiday on a farm forty miles up the Dee Valley in typical Highland scenery, when he was only seven or eight and recovering from scarlet fever.

At first Captain Byron had quartered himself with his wife, but she got on his nerves so much with her emotional moods, now loving, now furiously resentful, that he soon found his own lodgings at the other end of the street. For the moment he would stray no farther. Mrs. Byron might have little money, but who else in the world would spare him even a guinea? It was an absurd situation. When they could not meet without quarreling, he would write her notes or waylay her servant-girl, Agnes Gray, with inquiries in the street.

On one occasion the Captain asked to have the little boy for a visit. Mrs. Byron was pleased with this unusual paternal interest, but nervous about letting George pass into his hands. "Go on," counseled Agnes shrewdly, "if he keeps Master George one night he'll not want him for another!" Mrs. Byron tried the experiment. The infant was returned promptly the next day, and not asked for again.

In 1790 the Captain went off to France in search of livelier amusements than could be found in Aberdeen. The Revolution had just begun, but the massacres and executions were still to come. There was nothing to hinder Mad Jack in his favorite activities—making love to actresses and hotel maids, running up bills, and dodging his creditors.

His boy was not three when he saw his father for the last time, but he retained a vivid memory of the man and the "domestic broils" he witnessed when his parents were together. "He seemed born for his own ruin, and that of the other sex," Byron recalled in later years. He could scarcely have summed up his father in those terms at the time, but he may have been quite correct in feeling that the sight of those quarrels gave him a horror of marriage even at that tender age. If so, it was yet another illustration of the way in which childhood influences molded his own fate.

Within a year came the news that the Captain had died in France. Mrs. Byron had never ceased to love him, in spite of everything. Her hysterical cries of grief were audible in the street outside. She would never get over the shock, she blubbered. She found excuses for the Captain's most glaring misdeeds. Only necessity, not his own wish, she vowed, had driven the poor man from her side.

Now she had only their son to live for. Silly woman though she was, Mrs. Byron cared for the boy sincerely and did her best.

Nothing much could be done for his deformed right foot, though she never gave up hope, consulting doctors and surgeons continually, and paying for the treatment and appliances they recommended.

The boy was hardly a cripple. As he grew older he learned to box and was a spirited fighter. In England he played cricket, though (as is usual when a batsman has a temporary leg injury) he was allowed to have another boy run for him between the wickets. But it was natural that he should take most pleasure and pride in sports unaffected by his lameness, such as swimming and riding horseback and marksmanship. His earliest portrait shows him with bow and arrow at target practice—a seven-year-old boy in the clothes of the period, brief cutaway jacket, skin-tight pantaloons, and an immense lace collar, to which his hair falls in long curls like a Cavalier's. Later, pistol shooting took the place of archery.

His mother fussed over his limp and inevitably he became sensitive about it. Once Agnes was taking him for a walk when another woman paused to chat.

"What a pretty boy Byron is!" she commented. "What a pity he has such a leg!"

"Dinna speak of it!" the boy interrupted furiously in the broad Scots accent he had picked up in Aberdeen. And with an authentic flash of Byron wildness he lashed out at her with the toy whip he was carrying.

Now that she no longer had a husband cadging for money, Mrs. Byron could afford to keep up a slightly better home. She took an upstairs apartment at 64 Broad Street with three bedrooms, a kitchen, and a living room.

By the time he was five Byron had started school. A small figure in red jacket and trousers of buff-colored cotton, he would make his way down a narrow lane to the gloomy establishment in which a Mr. John Bowers instructed the small boys and girls of the neighborhood.

Here he learned to read and soon passed on to Latin grammar. In those days this subject was of immense—and absurd—importance. Education was based on Latin. Indeed, often it consisted of very little else. When he was seven he would enter the town's ancient grammar school, and without Latin he would be lost, for it filled the curriculum.

While Byron, still only six and a half, was battling with Latin declensions and conjugations, his mother learned something of more practical interest.

There had been a battle at Calvi in Corsica (Britain was now at war with the revolutionary government of France). This was the battle at which Nelson lost his eye. But it was also the battle in which the Wicked Lord lost his only grandson, killed by a cannon ball.

Lord Byron's three sons had all died before him. Now,

with the unexpected death of this young grandson, he would have no direct descendant to inherit his title and estates. If his nephew, Mad Jack, had lived a little longer, he would have been next in line.

By this unforeseen stroke of chance, the little boy in Aberdeen became "heir presumptive" to Newstead. That is to say, it could be "presumed" that he would inherit, but it was not absolutely certain. In theory the Wicked Lord might still marry again and have another son. But his age of seventy-two and his way of life made such an event improbable.

Mrs. Byron might be forgiven if, from this moment onwards, she began to think of her son as the sixth baron and to build some castles in the air.

Surely it could not be long before her George came into his inheritance, an inheritance that would solve all their financial troubles? It was a nuisance, of course, that the Wicked Lord was so peculiar and would have no dealings with his relatives. It was hard to discover any precise information—though she did her best, writing letters around the family and engaging a lawyer to keep his eye on her son's interests. It was common knowledge that the Newstead estate covered more than three thousand acres, and included not only the grounds of the Abbey and stretches of the old Sherwood Forest, but over a dozen farms, as well as quarries, lime kilns, and taverns, all of them presumably paying rent.

George meanwhile entered Aberdeen Grammar School and found the continual Latin lessons uninspiring. Even for handwriting the boys had to go over to a private school across the churchyard. As for ordinary reading, the schools of those days were not concerned with stimulating an in-

terest in modern literature. George, however, became an
avid reader in his spare time. Few books had yet been published for children, and those that existed were heavy with
moral instruction. George went straight to the books intended for his elders, and by the time he was ten he had a
formidable reading list behind him.

History and travel were his favorite subjects, especially
Roman history and tales of the East. He had started with
The Arabian Nights, and that led him on to books about
the Turks, who then ruled not only all the lands of what
we now call the Middle East but also Greece and much of
southeastern Europe. When he looked back on his childhood reading, Byron acknowledged how much it had in-
fluenced his decision to travel in that region and perhaps,
he added, "the oriental colouring which is observed in my
poetry."

Curiously enough, he hated poetry at this age.

So passed three years at the grammar school, and for all
his disability he held his own among the hundred and fifty
tough Scottish lads crammed into its tiny playground. His
lameness indeed made him aggressive. He was quick to
take offense and ever ready for a fight, but he could be a
warmhearted friend as well as a hot-tempered enemy.

He was soon old enough to understand his position as
his great-uncle's heir. Once, when his mother was enter-
taining a friend and quoting from a Parliamentary report
in the newspaper, the friend turned to the boy and said:
"Some day we shall have the pleasure of reading *your*
speeches in the House of Commons."

George answered smartly: "I hope not. If you read any
speeches of mine it will be in the House of Lords."

At that date the House of Lords was very much the

upper house of Parliament, not only in noble status but in real political power. It was not until the beginning of the twentieth century that the Commons, elected by democratic vote, asserted themselves as the true ruling body in Britain. In Byron's time no one doubted that a peer counted far more than a Member of Parliament.

One morning late in May, 1798, the news was broken to the boy. His mother must have known for some weeks that the Wicked Lord was dying, but she seems not to have prepared her son.

That morning, at roll call, when George's name was reached it was called in unfamiliar form.

"Dominus de Byron!"

Everyone stared. *Lord* Byron? George himself was so taken aback that he could not frame the single Latin word required in answer, *Adsum!* (Present!) He stood dumbfounded, and the tears rushed into his eyes.

The roll call was completed. The boys dispersed to their classes. The headmaster sent for George, greeted him with grave sympathy and (the boy noticed) with a new respect. His great-uncle had died. He was now himself "Lord Byron" and must be referred to as such. The headmaster offered him cake and a glass of wine, which probably helped to overcome the awkwardness of the occasion.

At home, George was embarrassed again. His mother chattered so much, telling the wonderful news to the neighbors. "Can you see any difference in me since I have been made a lord?" he demanded. "I perceive none myself."

Two or three months of formalities followed. Mrs. Byron wrote long letters to the lawyers and clucked indignantly when she was asked to produce documents, even the evidence of her own marriage to Mad Jack. There was the apartment to be given up, furniture to be sold, farewells made.

George left the grammar school forever when the summer holidays began. In August he mounted the south-bound coach with his mother, to claim at last the dreamed-of inheritance. Agnes had married some time before, and her sister May had taken her place as Mrs. Byron's only servant. May traveled with them. The expenses of the journey took half the money Mrs. Byron had obtained by selling her furniture.

What did that matter? Newstead, with its broad acres and its handsome Gothic priory mirrored in the lake, awaited them at the end of the road.

❧ 2 ❧

The Legacy of the
Wicked Lord

DISAPPOINTMENT also awaited them, although Newstead
was, and still is today, a place of enchantment.

Later, Byron was to describe it in *Don Juan:* "It stood
embosom'd in a happy valley,/Crown'd by high wood-
lands. . ."

Some of the old monastery buildings, notably the
church, were in ruins, "a glorious remnant of the Gothic
pile," with the stone tracery of "a mighty window," now
empty of stained glass, outlined like fretwork against the
open sky. But the monks' former living quarters ranged
around the cloisters, their refectory, parlor, chapter house,
and the like had for two and a half centuries served as the
home of the Byrons.

Other lines from *Don Juan* sketch the scene:

> Before the mansion lay a lucid lake,
> Broad as transparent, deep and freshly fed

By a river. . .

The woods sloped downwards to its brink, and stood
With their green faces fix'd upon the flood.
Its outlet dash'd into a deep cascade,
Sparkling with foam, until again subsiding. . .

Pursued its course, now gleaming, and now hiding
Its winding through the woods; now clear, now blue,
According as the skies their shadows threw.

All this beauty is still there to be seen, unspoiled, by
anyone driving the few miles out from the city of Nottingham, which now owns and looks after the estate.

The place Byron and his mother saw on that late August day in 1798 was different in one particular: it was desolate and neglected. The Wicked Lord had deliberately
let everything go to ruin, originally to revenge himself
upon his disobedient son, and, after that son's death, from
sheer malice against the family in general. He had made
up his mind that he would do his best to leave nothing
worth inheriting.

Mr. John Hanson, the lawyer, had traveled down from
London with his wife to meet the Byrons. He greeted
them sympathetically. Mrs. Byron could see for herself
that it was impossible to stay at Newstead. She must drive
on to Nottingham and stay with relatives. The boy and his
mother gazed around them in horror. Someone had been
keeping cattle in the entrance hall and parlor. The great
refectory looked like a hayloft. Everywhere the roof
seemed to have leaked. It was said that the Wicked Lord
had died in the only room that did not let in the rain.

All this could be put right eventually, but it would cost

money, immense sums of money. For the moment there *was* no money. The Wicked Lord had lain unburied for nearly a month after his death until enough could be found to pay for the funeral. Of course, there was the estate. He had cut down the trees and done everything he could to ruin it, but he could not destroy the land. In time, with patience, economy, and good management, the estate could be made profitable again. But it would take years.

The boy, limping through this moldy splendor, could not fully understand the anxious murmurings of his mother and the London lawyer. "It was a change," he recalled afterwards, "from a shabby Scotch flat to a palace." This was his heritage, his very own. It was sad that they had to leave it as soon as their inspection was finished, and drive on to Nottingham.

Mr. Hanson was sensible, Mrs. Byron obstinate. In the end she compromised.

She would move into a corner of the Abbey and make it habitable. Hanson, from his London office in Chancery Lane, would try to unravel the legal complications, which were considerable. For one thing, the Wicked Lord had sold the other valuable family estate at Rochdale in Lancashire. Now it must be proved that he had had no right to do so. The Rochdale property must be won back for the new heir. As for Newstead, Hanson urged, they must find a rich tenant for the next few years, one who could afford to put it in good order and leave it as a home fit for Byron to occupy when he grew up.

The boy himself loved Newstead from the beginning.

There was a great wolfhound named Woolly, with whom he made friends, and a pony on which he rode around with Mr. Hanson to be introduced to the local gentry. He began to feel that he really *was* a lord. Solemnly he planted a young oak tree in the grounds to commemorate his arrival. Sometimes he played with his great-uncle's pistols and the fateful sword that had killed Chaworth. He knew all about that quarrel. There was a girl named Mary Chaworth living at Annesley Hall nearby. She was two years older than he. "Here is a pretty young lady," said the lawyer teasingly. "You had better marry her." "What, Mr. Hanson," the boy retorted, "the Capulets and Montagues intermarry?"

Hanson had all his other business to see to, and could not spend long at Newstead. Mrs. Byron had too much on her mind to give her son continual attention. And, to tell the truth, the boy was apt to be a nuisance, playing the young lord and plaguing Owen Mealey, the new caretaker-gardener, with demands the poor man could not cope with, struggling as he was to run the place alone.

It therefore seemed better that Byron should spend most of his time in Nottingham, nine miles away. For some of that time he lodged with May in a house still marked by a tablet, at the top of St. James Street, a narrow lane leading up from the market place to the sandstone cliff occupied by the castle.

Nottingham was then a beautiful town of elegant Georgian houses, mingled with gabled inns and other buildings of an earlier period. Industry was creeping in, but steam power had not arrived with all its smoke and noise. The people manufactured stockings and similar goods, mostly in their own homes, and from countless long windows in red-brick cottages was heard the characteristic *shee-shee-chockerty-chock* of their hand-operated knitting frames. All around the little town still lay the unspoiled open country. One way, the meadows stretched to the River Trent, dotted in spring with thousands of wild crocuses. The other way, towards Newstead, a splendid line of windmills stood along the skyline, and the low hills rolled away in waves to the distant remnants of Sherwood Forest.

Nottingham was a gay, violent, rebellious town, with a lot of the Robin Hood spirit still in its people. From time to time the great market place became a battleground over one question or another—anything from the French Revolution to the high price of cheese was enough to arouse the inhabitants and bring the Dragoons or Hussars galloping from their barracks, sabers in hand.

"I have lived seventeen years in the town," lamented one gentleman, in the very year that Byron arrived there, "and during that time there have been seventeen riots." When he grew up, Byron himself referred in a letter to "that political pandemonium, Nottingham." Nothing very alarming, however, seems to have happened while he was at 76 St. James Street. The worst feature, probably, was the behavior of May Gray.

Unsupervised by Mrs. Byron, and far from her native Scotland and all the people who knew her, the maid seems to have gone completely to pieces. She went drinking in the low alehouses, got into bad company, and either stayed out late, leaving the boy to go to bed when he thought fit, or brought highly unsuitable visitors into their lodgings. It is hard to say whether her absence or her presence had the worse effect on the boy. Sometimes she beat him, at others she was objectionable in her affectionate familiarities.

Probably this girl did lasting psychological harm to Byron and helped to give him that strangely mixed-up attitude towards the opposite sex destined to complicate his life so painfully when he grew up.

One of his mother's reasons for leaving him in Nottingham was to secure some remedial treatment for his foot. This was arranged with a Mr. Lavender, who called himself a surgeon but was merely a maker of surgical appliances for the hospital across the road. This man's idea of treatment was to rub the twisted foot with oil and then clamp it painfully into a wooden device in the hope of straightening it. Byron soon suspected Lavender's ignorance. Once he wrote out some jumbled, meaningless syllables to look like words, showed them to the quack, and asked him what language they were. "Italian," said Lavender, who thought it bad business ever to admit that there was something he did not know. Byron's roar of laughter did not improve their relationship.

Mrs. Byron thought a good deal about her son's foot but not much about his mind, for she was uneducated herself and had only the dimmest notion of intellectual matters.

It was Byron himself who had to write to her and point out that he had received no schooling since he left Aberdeen and would soon have forgotten all he had ever learned. He suggested that he might have lessons with a Mr. Dummer Rogers, an American living in Nottingham on a British pension because he had taken the British side during the struggle for independence. Mr. Rogers was already tutor to Byron's girl cousins in the town, but could easily give him separate lessons in the evening.

"If some plan of this kind is not adopted," Byron warned his mother, "I shall be branded with the name of a dunce, which you know I could never bear."

Mrs. Byron finally agreed, and for several months Byron read Vergil and Cicero and took other lessons with the American, who proved a sympathetic teacher. It used to worry him to see Byron with his foot screwed up in Lavender's horrible contraption.

"My lord," he said one day, "I don't feel comfortable at having you sitting opposite me there, in such pain as you must be."

"Never mind, Mr. Rogers," the boy answered, "you shall not see any signs of it in me."

Such arrangements could be only temporary. Byron must go to school again, have his foot examined by a London specialist, and meet the Earl of Carlisle, his father's cousin, who had been made his guardian. So in July, 1799, a little less than a year after coming down from Scotland, the boy set out for London with Hanson. His mother did not go, but, to his annoyance, she sent May Gray to look after him.

The eighteenth century was just going out, the nineteenth waiting to begin. The French Revolution had given place to the domination of a single man, Napoleon Bonaparte, who that summer was fighting a campaign in Egypt with the dream of breaking through to India. Pitt, the British Prime Minister, had lined up his country with Russia, Austria, Turkey, and other allies to oppose the French. Nelson had just defeated a French fleet and become Baron Nelson of the Nile, but few people had yet heard of the man who, as the Duke of Wellington, would finally break Napoleon at Waterloo sixteen years later. At that moment, the future duke was a little-known commander in India, skillfully preparing the discomfiture of Napoleon should he ever appear in that distant country. George Washington had accepted reappointment as Commander in Chief in the United States and was preparing for the sad possibility that he might have to fight America's late friends, the French, but he was to die suddenly before the end of that year, and the necessity did not arise.

Jane Austen had been quietly writing *Pride and Prejudice* and *Northanger Abbey,* though neither novel would be published for some time. Wordsworth and Coleridge had just combined to publish the *Lyrical Ballads,* destined to set English poetry on a new course, although the book was given a poor welcome at first.

It was the period, roughly, that we call Regency, though in strict historical fact the Prince of Wales was not Regent until some years later. His father, George III, had recovered from his first attack of what was then regarded as insanity, but which recent research suggests was a rare ailment, not madness at all, and tragically misunderstood by the poor King's doctors at the time. At all events, the King was again ruling the country whose crown he had worn for nearly forty years, but he was a man of simple country tastes, preferring Windsor to London, and smart society looked to his son to take the lead in matters of taste and fashion, whether from his town mansion, Carlton House, or his seaside home, the fantastical Brighton Pavilion.

So the London to which the coach was carrying young Byron in that last summer of the eighteenth century was already in essence the city we think of as Regency London —a place of flat-faced brick houses with sash windows, pillared doorways, and elegant wrought-iron railings, of green parks and squares, and of white churches; a city loud with clopping hoofs and spinning carriage wheels and the sweetly plaintive cries of street vendors; a city still of great beauty despite its many trades and its million inhabitants, which three years later was to inspire Wordsworth as he paused on Westminster Bridge in the early hours:

Earth has not anything to show more fair: . . .

And to go on:

This City now doth, like a garment, wear
The beauty of the morning; . . .

That year the Prince's friend, Beau Brummell, came into a fortune and set up his elegant bachelor headquarters in Mayfair, laying down standards of dress and etiquette to which even the Prince conformed. Gentlemen's fashions themselves emphasized the break between two centuries. The full knee breeches, silk stockings, and buckled shoes became an archaic ceremonial uniform. Men squeezed their legs into tight buckskin breeches that ended in high boots, or drew on equally narrow, knitted pantaloons buttoning at the ankle. Top hats replaced the three-cornered type.

Byron was not heading for Beau Brummell's Mayfair, but a sufficiently fashionable district at Kensington where the Hansons lived. There might be cows and cornfields—it was two miles from Piccadilly—but there was elegance too, though it was a long time since Kensington Palace had been occupied by a monarch. A foreign visitor at this time described Kensington as "a lovely village full of wealthy people."

The Hanson children, three boys and a girl, were warm in their welcome. They must have discussed their guest beforehand, for seven-year-old Mary Anne cried out in surprise: "But he is a *pretty* boy!" Byron was soon at home with them all. Although he liked to lie on the sofa in the mornings, lost in his book, he was always ready to throw it down and join in a game.

The meeting with Lord Carlisle went badly. The Earl tried to be friendly, but Byron was awkward and rude. Nor was the visit to the specialist a happy occasion. Dr. Baillie shook his head over the deformed foot. If treated properly at the start, it might have been cured. Now that the boy was eleven, it was too late. Shortly after this, Byron was fitted with a special boot, and there were no more hopeless attempts to twist his foot into normality.

After six weeks with the Hansons, Byron was sent to a small private boarding school at Dulwich, some miles south of the city, which was run by a Scot, Dr. Glennie. As he had feared, he was a long way behind the other boys in Latin grammar, and, when he made the mistake of standing too much on his dignity, they laughed and nicknamed him the Old English Baron. Perhaps it was to protect him from too much teasing at first, or because Hanson had asked for him to be given a room to himself, that he was given a bed in the headmaster's study, where he enjoyed the run of the books. He was always impatient of set lessons and drudgery, but he had a passion for reading so long as he could please himself.

He spent the Christmas holidays with the Hansons at

Kensington—or rather with the Hanson children, who had been left in the care of an aunt while their parents paid a long visit to Mrs. Byron at Newstead. The dates did not fit those of the school holidays, and Mrs. Byron seems not to have been dying to see her son, nor he her. He was much happier with the young Hanson tribe, especially now that May Gray had returned to his mother. They got up to all kinds of tricks in those Christmas holidays, sometimes trespassing into the forbidden territory of the servants' quarters and teasing the cook, "a fiery and violent old woman," as one of the Hanson boys recalled in later life. Once she chased after Byron with some murderous kitchen implement in her hand, shouting: "You a lord! I wonder who the devil ever made *you* a lord!"

Mrs. Byron came down with the Hansons just before school began again. Byron was delighted to find that his plea had been granted—May had been paid off and sent back to Scotland. But his satisfaction was probably mixed with a sense of guilt, for he not only sent her parting presents (the proper thing to do, as he must have been taught), but afterwards wrote to her from time to time. It is a common experience to have mixed feelings in such cases. If May had been cruel she had also been kind, and the two of them had been very close, perhaps too close in the period when he was otherwise lonely and neglected.

His mother was another woman towards whom his feelings were mixed.

She was, as always, temperamental and impulsive. Sometimes she was fussily affectionate. Sometimes she would fly into a temper and box his ears or slap his hands. Byron was going through a spell of nail-biting, like many another boy of his age subjected to anxieties and strains. Like many another parent before and since, Mrs. Byron reacted with angry impatience.

Byron went back to Dr. Glennie's school, and his mother settled in lodgings near Sloane Square, where she became a nuisance to all concerned.

She would appear at Dulwich on a Saturday and carry off her son for the entire weekend, occasionally keeping him for the whole of the following week as well. Naturally, his schoolwork suffered. Hanson had to instruct the headmaster to forbid these absences unless there was written permission from the Earl of Carlisle. When this was not given, Mrs. Byron's reaction may be imagined. She caused such a storm that she could be heard by the servants and pupils all over the school. One boy said bluntly afterwards: "Byron, your mother is a fool." And for once Byron, normally loyal in face of the outside world and ever ready to fight for the family honor, could only answer miserably: "I know."

The Earl knew it too. He had never wanted to be Byron's guardian. He was a good-natured man, but he seemed unable to make real contact with the boy. The mother was impossible. "I can have nothing more to do with Mrs. Byron," he told Hanson, "you must now manage her as you can."

Hanson did his best. It must have been for the boy's sake, not for his lawyer's fees. Sorting out the tangled Byron affairs brought more headaches than guineas. But Hanson divined some special quality in this awkward boy with his alternate outbursts of fun and fury. His mind was not to be measured by his backwardness in Latin.

Again Byron spent happy Christmas holidays with the Hansons in Kensington. Back at school, he was told he must make an extra effort to improve his work. There was a reason. Gleefully he wrote off to a cousin: "I am going to leave this damned place at Easter and am going to Harrow."

❧ 3 ❧

Latin or Love?

HARROW, then as now, was paired with Eton in the eyes of the English upper class. To one school or the other went most of the young nobility, along with the sons of the wealthy and the influential.

If Byron was to take his place in society when he grew up, it was vital for him to pass through one of these schools. In the House of Lords, in the fashionable clubs, in the great country houses, his future companions would be mostly Old Etonians or Old Harrovians. He must learn to "speak the same language"—literally, since he still had traces of Aberdeen in his speech, but mainly in the sense that he must acquire the manners and thought processes, perhaps the prejudices, of the English ruling caste. He must make the friendships that would help him in later life and compensate him for his odd upbringing and previous isolation from the families of his own rank.

Byron went to Harrow at thirteen and stayed until the summer of 1805, when he was seventeen and a half.

The school stood on a hill, eleven miles north of London. It was then a tall building, in shape not unlike one of those Norman castles that consist of a single massive keep. Drawing nearer, however, the new boy saw that there were no battlements, but small gables and a belfry, on the top, windows rather than arrow slits, and a playground instead of a courtyard below. The place was certainly old. It had been opened in 1611. To that date belongs the still-existing Fourth Form room, its panels carved with names famous in English history. Byron was to cut his own name there on the day he left, in the year of the Battle of Trafalgar.

The boys wore tall black hats, tail coats, and tight trousers. They lived in houses supervised by various masters. Byron was placed in the care of Henry Drury, son of the headmaster, Dr. Drury. He always liked this headmaster, who was, he wrote, "the most amiable clergyman I ever knew," a scholar and a gentleman. "What little I have learnt I owe to him alone, nor is it his fault that it was not more."

With Mr. Drury, his housemaster, relations were less happy. After two years, Byron was writing to his mother in furious indignation. He had been caught talking in church. He admitted that was wrong. But Mr. Drury, without saying a word to him, had taken the other boy aside afterwards, called Byron a blackguard, and said that he deserved to be expelled. Byron refused to have such things said behind his back. Yes, he had talked in church and he had been idle, but he had done nothing mean or dishonorable. "If I am treated in this manner," wrote the boy, "I will not stay at this school."

He stayed, but the four years were stormy, and in his

final period even the "amiable" headmaster was driven to
rebuke him. Even though he was about to leave Harrow,
it was no reason "to make the house a scene of riot and
confusion." Generally speaking, though, he was happier in
the second half of his Harrow career than in the first. "I
do not dislike Harrow," he wrote at the time, "I find ways
and means to amuse myself very pleasantly there."

The lessons were a dismal grind of Latin and Greek.
Not for another generation or two would other subjects,
such as modern languages, English literature, or the history of his own country, become a standard feature of the
curriculum. It is understandable that an intelligent boy
saw little point in lessons so remote from the age he lived
in. But there was another life outside the classroom. He
enjoyed the swimming, though he had to hire a pony because it was a long walk to the bathing place, and he became a good cricketer. He was picked to play for the
school in the annual match against Eton, a traditional
event that still takes place.

There were many fights in his first years, but there were
also friendships. The second Hanson boy, Hargreaves, had
gone to Harrow at the same time, but Byron was never de-
pendent on him. He made his own way. His friends included young noblemen like the Duke of Dorset and the
Earl of Clare, Robert Peel (a future Prime Minister), and
others with humbler prospects, such as William Harness, a
smaller boy, lame like himself, whom he defended against
bullying. He always remained friends with Harness, who
became a clergyman.

School holidays were spent in various places, sometimes
with the Hansons, sometimes with his mother. She took

him to Bath, where she had first met and fallen in love
with his father, and to the spa at Cheltenham. From this
resort they visited the Malvern Hills, which they could see
in the distance, standing up dramatically from the field-
and-orchard patchwork of the wide Severn Vale. These
hills, with their headlong slopes and outcrops of rock, reminded him of the Scottish Highlands, and he was suddenly homesick. "After I returned to Cheltenham," he
confessed in later years, "I used to watch them every afternoon at sunset, with a sensation that I cannot describe.
This was boyish enough: but I was then only thirteen
years of age. . ."

Newstead was now tenanted by young Lord Grey de
Ruthyn, who was to live there until Byron was twenty-
one. Mrs. Byron took a house some miles away, Burgage
Manor, at the end of the main street in Southwell, a quiet
little market town with a splendid Norman minister and
very little else.

Byron found the place dull. Also, he avoided his mother's company as much as he could. As Lord Grey had invited him to visit Newstead whenever he liked, he took
the tenant at his word. To begin with, Lord Grey was
himself absent, so Byron stayed with Mealey, the gardener,
making himself a nuisance again with his requirements.

Among these was the daily grooming of his lordship's
horse, so that Byron could visit Annesley Hall and ride
with Mary Chaworth, the girl Hanson had teased him
about several years before.

The situation was now very different. Byron was fifteen
and a half, and there had been one or two cases already
when his interest in girls had been aroused, though there

had been little chance for any affair to develop. Mary was seventeen, but that did not matter: he was attracted to girls older than himself. She was already engaged to a young sporting squire in the neighborhood, John Musters, but in his absence she was glad of another good-looking escort. Byron, she could have explained, was still at school, and was her distant cousin. Perhaps she was not quite so innocent. Perhaps she enjoyed the guilty pleasure of a mild flirtation that she never took seriously.

Byron's feelings were deeper. One day, with others, they made a longer excursion into the Derbyshire hills. He never forgot that expedition. They visited a cavern with an underground river. The rock hung so low over the water that tourists had to lie, two at a time, in a small boat pushed by the wading guide. "The companion of my transit was M.A.C., with whom I had been long in love, and never told it, though *she* had discovered it without. I recollect my sensations, but cannot describe them—and it is as well."

He made up a story that he had met a "bogle," or ghost, when riding back to Newstead after dark. This led, as he intended, to an invitation to stay at Annesley. The time came for him to return to Harrow. He did not go. His mother explained in a letter to Hanson: "I cannot get him to return to school, though I have done all in my power for six weeks past. . . The boy is distractedly in love with Miss Chaworth, and he has . . . spent all his time at Annesley."

Only the girl herself could end the matter, and she did, perhaps by accident. The story goes (it may not be true) that one night Byron overheard Mary talking to her maid.

"What, me care for that lame boy?" Furious and humili-
ated, he dashed from the house and galloped back to Newstead through the autumn darkness.

His mother had already conceded that he should not return to Harrow until the New Year. He stayed at the
Abbey, where Lord Grey was by now in residence. For a
time the young man and the boy were close friends, and
used to go out shooting in the moonlight. In January
there was a mysterious quarrel between them, which
ended that friendship too, and prevented his visiting Newstead so long as Grey rented it. "I am not reconciled to
Lord Grey," he wrote, *"and I never will. . .* My reasons
for ceasing that friendship are such as I cannot explain,
not even to you. . ."

This was in a letter addressed to Augusta Byron, the
daughter of his father's earlier marriage to the divorced
Marchioness of Carmarthen. He had met his half sister for
the first time only a year or two before and had seldom
seen her since, though the two of them now kept up an affectionate correspondence.

Someone described Augusta about this time as "very
pretty" with "a very fine head of dark brown hair," beautiful eyes, and a fine complexion though rather freckled.
She was "light as a feather" and "very striking" in general
appearance. She was almost four years older than her half
brother.

Theirs was an odd relationship, fated to play a crucial
part in Byron's life.

They were drawn together because they had had the
same father, and they sentimentalized the memory of that
not very admirable parent because neither had much else
in the form of family loyalty to cling to. Augusta had lost

her mother at birth and had grown up as an orphan in
various noble families. Byron had *his* mother, but that did
not always seem to him the blessing it should have been.
In his childhood she had deliberately prevented any contact with Augusta, who had shown an elder sister's normal
interest in the progress of "Baby Byron." It was only because Augusta got on well with the Earl of Carlisle, and
Mrs. Byron thought she would be useful in that way, that
the two young people were allowed to meet in the boy's
early days at Harrow.

Thus they met as strangers. They had none of the com-
monplace memories of brother and sister who grow up in
the same home, playing and quarreling, sharing jokes and
germs, knowing each other so familiarly that there can
never be any room for romance or mystery in their relationship.

Even now their meetings were rare. But they could ex-
change letters. And although at first Augusta complained
that her young brother was a neglectful letter writer, this
changed after his disappointment over Mary Chaworth. In
his loneliness and boredom during the holidays at Southwell, he poured out his heart to his "dearest Augusta,"
telling her she was "the only relation I have who treats me
as a friend."

To Augusta alone he could speak frankly about the
"outrageous" behavior of his mother, who was continually
flying into rages and vilifying not only himself but their
dead father and the whole Byron connection. Mrs. Byron
did not encourage all this correspondence and he preferred to write when she was out of the house. A typical
letter begins: "My dearest Augusta, I seize this interval
of my *amiable* mother's absence this afternoon. . ." Au-

gusta, always gentle and peace-loving, did not encourage his outbursts. She was a restraining influence, trying whenever she could, through Lord Carlisle or Hanson, to keep her young brother out of trouble.

In his final weeks at Harrow, when he had been chosen to recite a dramatic passage at the Speech Day ceremony, he sent her just the sort of humorous letter that any schoolboy might write, anxious to show off a beautiful elder sister to his friends—and himself to that sister. He warned her to bring a gentleman as escort, "as I shall be too much engaged all the morning to take care of you, and I should not imagine you would admire *stalking* about by yourself." She should come early, so that he could secure her a good place. She was staying in London with Lord Carlisle, so he begged her to make her appearance "in one of his Lordship's most *dashing* carriages, as our Harrow etiquette admits of nothing but the most *superb* vehicles, on our Grand Festivals." He implored her, "for God's sake bring as few women with you as possible," and ended, "believe me, dearest Augusta, your affectionate brother, Byron."

The use of the surname, so curious to modern ears, was normal at the time. Englishmen scarcely used their first names. Shelley was "Shelley" even to his wife.

Augusta seems not to have managed the visit, but one feels sure that she was just as disappointed as Byron.

⊱ 4 ⊰

Wild Oats

Byron had hoped to go on to Oxford, where most of his closest school friends would be. But no rooms were available at Christ Church, the college fashionable with the nobility, and to his vexation he had to go to Cambridge.

They were the only two universities in England, and neither was like any university today.

The Cambridge Byron entered in October, 1805, was a little country town, a day's drive from London by stagecoach, and so sleepy during the long summer vacation that the grass sprang up greenly between the cobbles of the main streets.

Dotted through this town were sixteen quite separate colleges, large and small, each with its own gate, chapel, dining hall, and other buildings ranged around a court, and each run by its own group of Fellows, who, so long as they were clergymen of the Church of England and did not marry, could draw their money and do as little work as they liked until the day they died.

These colleges made up the university. Byron was admitted to the largest and grandest of them, Trinity College, which had the same social status as Christ Church at Oxford. It was one of a row of half a dozen that ran down to the River Cam behind and had footbridges across to the gardens—the combination of splendid buildings, ancient trees, smooth-shaven lawns, and vivid splashes of flowers and shrubs that is still known simply as the Backs and is the glory of Cambridge.

Everything about Trinity was palatial. Byron liked that. The hall where he dined, with its hammer beams, stained glass, and wainscoting, was served by a kitchen as spacious and lofty as the nave of a cathedral. As for his own quarters, he wrote to Augusta:

"I am now most pleasantly situated in superexcellent rooms, flanked on one side by my Tutor, upon the other by an old Fellow, both of whom are rather checks on my vivacity. I am allowed five hundred [pounds] a year, a servant and horse, so feel as independent as a German prince who coins his own cash, or a Cherokee chief who coins no cash at all, but enjoys what is more precious, Liberty."

He might well feel free. Not much work was expected of anyone: a young man could slip painlessly through university though he scarcely attended a lecture or opened a book. Examinations were a formality. Degrees were awarded merely for remaining in Cambridge the requisite three years. Nor did a degree matter, except to a poor man who would have to earn his living as a schoolmaster or clergyman. Others could quit the university as soon as it bored them, and many treated it simply as a finishing school, a place in which to acquire an extra polish and enjoy themselves with their friends until they were twenty-one.

Discipline was light, provided one did not look for trouble—as Shelley did, when he was expelled from Oxford a few years later. The Fellows, or "dons," were often snobs who hesitated to take action against students of rank or riches. A young nobleman like Byron had special privileges and wore a gown with gold trimming to show that he must be treated with more respect than anyone who was merely a brilliant scholar.

Once, when Byron came up against a college rule he could not break (a ban on dogs), he found his own way of asserting his independence. There was no rule against keeping bears, so he bought one and took it for walks on a chain. What, he was asked, did he mean to do with the animal? "He shall sit for a fellowship," said Byron nonchalantly. The bear was allowed to stay for a time and was then sent to Newstead.

At Cambridge Byron could lead the carefree life of a gentleman. He had his own rooms, furnished to his own taste. His gilded four-poster bed, with its coronets and original hangings, may still be seen at Newstead. He had his college servant, or "gyp," as they are called at Cambridge. And, though he had still more than three years to wait before he came of age, he had a generous allowance fixed by the legal settlement and paid regularly by Hanson. One of his first purchases on arriving at the age of seventeen and a half was four dozen bottles of port, sherry, claret, and madeira. Schooldays were over.

In fact, though there were times in his life when Byron drank far more than was good for him (as almost every gentleman did in those days), he also went through long periods of abstinence when little but soda water passed his lips. With food, too, he was usually sparing. He was anxious to keep his weight down, and every day he liked to take some strenuous exercise, riding, swimming, boxing or fencing, as the case might be.

His usual companion was Edward Noel Long, who had come up with him from Harrow. They vied with each other in diving, throwing plates and even coins into the dim green waters of the Cam where it was fourteen feet deep, and fetching them up from the bed. By a tragic coincidence, Long was drowned a few years later, when he was serving in the Guards and was sailing to Lisbon to fight in the Peninsular War.

There were, of course, no girl students then, and as the college dons might not marry, there were no daughters to brighten the Cambridge scene. It was an all-male community. Some undergraduates might carry on secret love affairs with girls from the inns and shops of the town, but most of them contented themselves, as Byron did, with the close and affectionate friendships they formed with each other.

In the latter part of his time at Cambridge, Byron was one of a lively quartet.

One of them, John Cam Hobhouse, who became his lifelong and most trusted friend, began by disliking him but swung around when he discovered that Byron wrote poetry.

Another, Charles Skinner Matthews, a friend of Hobhouse's, had been allowed to use Byron's rooms when he was away. On being shown into them, he was warned by the tutor, "Mr. Matthews, I recommend to your attention not to damage any of the movables. For Lord Byron, sir, is a young man of *tumultuous passions.*" This phrase delighted Matthews' sense of humor, and, so long as he occupied the rooms, he would repeat the warning to everyone who came in, begging them to treat even the door with caution. He was curious to know more about the "young man of tumultuous passions," and when Byron came back a warm friendship began. Matthews was a brilliant scholar and an amusing talker. He too was drowned a few years afterwards, bathing alone amid the treacherous reeds of the Cam. Byron, who so loved swimming and whose name is still given to his favorite pool at Grantchester, seemed to be haunted by such tragedies among his friends.

The last of the group, Scrope Davies, was already a Fellow of King's College, but this responsible position did not prevent his gambling regularly in London and going about with Beau Brummell's dandified set. He had a keen mind too, and a quick repartee matching that of Matthews, and he was glad enough to turn from the dull company of the high table dons to the more stimulating society of Matthews and his friends. He was good for Byron. His sharp common sense could deflate the young peer's sense of his own importance. When Byron in a tantrum, hoping to impress them, declaimed dramatically, "I shall go *mad!*" Davies quietly remarked, "It is much more like silliness than madness." He was another loyal friend to Byron, and in later years once lent him nearly five thousand pounds.

Byron had grand ideas. The humiliating poverty of his childhood made him doubly determined to appear lavish. He set up a carriage and four, kept two fine saddle horses, Brighton and Sultan, and during his vacations collected various dogs—his beloved Boatswain, the Newfoundland, whose grave is to be seen at Newstead, a ferocious bulldog, Nelson, which had to be shot quickly when it attacked a horse, and its replacement, another bulldog, named Smut, the college ban on which led to the purchase of the bear.

Then, too, he had to employ a groom and a valet. When the latter stole from him, Byron had the expense of prosecuting him; and then, stricken with remorse when the man received the sentence of seven years' transportation to Australia, further legal costs in trying to secure him a royal pardon.

There were the college bills, clothes, and countless other items. He even bought books, and read them, unlike many of the emptier-headed young gentlemen around him. When donations were invited for a statue to the memory of Pitt, the statesman, Byron must outdo the others with a lordly gift of thirty guineas he could not afford.

Such extravagance led him into trouble all-round.

He was rude to poor Hanson, who could not send him money beyond what he was entitled to. Byron later apologized.

His mother thought, with some reason, that he was going the same ruinous way his father had gone. There was a danger she might come storming up to Cambridge. Byron warned Hanson: "The instant I hear of her arrival I quit Cambridge, though expulsion be the consequence."

He avoided staying with her at Southwell as much as he could. He "dreaded the approach of the vacations as the harbingers of misery." But if he had no money to go to London or elsewhere, he was forced to pass those months at home. At one point he could not even return to Cambridge because of his unpaid college bills.

He fell out even with Augusta. He had turned to her
for help. He had been to moneylenders, but they would
not accept his signature because he was under twenty-one.
Augusta was of age. Would she put *her* name to the paper?
The girl was deeply worried. She said she would rather
give him the money herself, but this he proudly refused.
She did not know what to do for the best, and consulted
Hanson—and, worse still, the Earl of Carlisle. Byron was
furious, and there was a long gap in the affectionate correspondence with "dearest Augusta," whom he felt to be in
league with his enemies. And about this time, in 1807, she
married her cousin, Colonel George Leigh, a fact which
gave Byron no pleasure but rather a pang of unreasonable
jealousy.

When Augusta would not sign the moneylender's guaran-
tee, Byron turned to a London hotel proprietress, who
obliged by putting her name to it.

He was spending much of his time, when he ought to
have been at Cambridge or at home, staying at one hotel
or another in Piccadilly, Bond Street, or Albemarle Street.

Neither his guardian, nor Hanson, nor any older and
soberer person, had any influence over him, and perhaps
nobody made the hopeless attempt to steer him. Byron
went his own willful way, scorning the dullness of respect-
ability. He ran around with professional boxers and girls
of bad reputation. One such girl he took to Brighton, the
seaside town which the Prince of Wales was making fashionable. Byron dressed her as a boy and passed her off as
his own imaginary brother, "Gordon."

A mixture of reasons drove him to this wildness. One
side of him was unconventional: he enjoyed shocking peo-

ple. Another side of him was just as conventional: a young gentleman was expected to sow his wild oats, a young lord especially, a young Byron most of all. In this respect Byron was secretly eager to do what was expected of him. The shadow of Aberdeen still lay upon him. Just because he had grown up poor and unknown, he was always doubly anxious to conform to the accepted idea of an aristocrat. He was self-conscious and insecure.

Men like Hanson and the Earl of Carlisle and many others, right up to the poor old King himself, represented the solid, moral part of the nation and shook their heads over such goings-on. But Byron was not at all unusual in his behavior. If anyone had criticized him, he could have pointed out that the Prince of Wales and most of the King's other sons led scandalous private lives, that leading statesmen like Charles James Fox had been notorious drinkers and gamblers, and that Nelson, the dead hero of Trafalgar, had left his own wife to live with Lady Hamilton.

So Byron was the product of English upper-class society in that age; and also of his Byron and Gordon blood, his neglected upbringing, and of various early experiences, such as his humiliation by Mary Chaworth, that had twisted his nature as harmfully as his foot.

He had felt tender, romantic love for a girl of his own kind—and where had it led him? He turned now to girls of another sort, girls who did not involve his deepest feelings, who were out for what they could get, who were amusing for a time but could be discarded when they grew tiresome. Girls, in short, who knew their place, as they did in the East. From childhood Byron had been fascinated by the Orient, that exotic world where sultans and pashas ruled unchallenged in their gorgeous palaces, with whole harems of beautiful women to be petted and punished at will. A man there did not worry his head about a woman's feelings. He did as he pleased. The fantasy appealed to Byron. True, he was no sultan, but he had a title and money, even if the money was borrowed, and these gave him power. This was London, not Baghdad, but in London money bought people as well as things. In those hectic months he almost wore himself out, trying to relive the adventures of *The Arabian Nights.*

There was more to Byron than this, or he would be forgotten by now, along with the numerous other young men who were running wild in London at the same time.

For years he had been writing poetry. Mostly it was the sentimental, exaggerated stuff many boys churn out and blush to read again in later years. Byron's early efforts show little signs of genius.

Nonetheless, as early as 1806, when he was eighteen, he arranged for a collection of his verses to be printed in Newark, the next town to Southwell, for private circulation among his friends. Some of these poems were outspokenly passionate. A local clergyman friend, shown an advance copy, was shocked by them, and Byron was persuaded to destroy the whole edition before sending them out: in fact, just four copies exist today. In the following January a revised collection, entitled *Poems and Various Occasions,* was actually sent out to his friends. Some of their comments were so encouraging that Byron arranged for the same local printer to bring out a public edition, under the altered title of *Hours of Idleness,* and by March, 1807, this was on sale in the bookshops. It included some lines he had written just after Mary Chaworth's marriage:

Hills of Annesley, bleak and barren,
Where my thoughtless childhood stray'd,
How the northern tempests, warring,
Howl above thy tufted shade!

Now no more, the hours beguiling;
Former favourite haunts I see;
Now no more my Mary smiling
Makes ye seem a heaven to me.

Such verses (many written, like these, while he was still at school) did not make any great stir. But in offering them not just to his personal friends, but to the general public, Byron had taken a risk. He had planted a time bomb for himself, which did not explode until twelve months afterwards.

The explosion took the form of a criticism in the *Edinburgh Review,* a quarterly magazine of great prestige among the intellectuals.

As was common in those days, the critic did not put a signature to his article, but he was in fact a brilliant and immensely ambitious Scotsman named Henry Brougham, afterwards Lord Chancellor of England. At this date, not quite thirty, he was still carving his own career with merciless strokes of his powerful wit. He made no allowance for Byron's youth, but attacked him with heavy sarcasm. Self-made himself (he achieved his own peerage many years later), he was obviously jealous of Byron's inherited title, indicating that, if he had not been *Lord* Byron, no one would have noticed his poems. He could see no promise in them. The young author had better give up poetry and do something more useful. "His effusions are spread over a dead flat, and can no more get above or below the level, than if they were so much stagnant water."

Byron was shattered. For months, like any other beginner, he had frankly enjoyed seeing his book in the shop windows and reading notices in the papers. He wrote to Hobhouse:

"As an author, I am cut to atoms by the E. Review. It is just out, and has completely demolished my little fabric of fame."

He told his mother never to mention his poetry to him again. He had finished with it forever. It had been all right for a schoolboy, but as a man he wished to forget it.

This mood quickly passed. "I regret that Mrs. Byron is so much annoyed," he told another friend. "For my own part, these 'paper bullets of the brain' have only taught me to stand fire." His lasting emotion was anger and a desire for revenge. The review, he said in later years, "knocked me down—but I got up again."

His revenge took the form of a long poem, *English Bards and Scotch Reviewers,* in which he showed that he could be as savage as anyone. Wrongly imagining that the anonymous review had been written by a man named Francis Jeffrey, he compared him with the notorious hanging judge, Jeffreys. In other passages he attacked most of the leading poets of the day—Wordsworth, Southey, Coleridge, and Scott. His gibes were not always fair. Afterwards, he regretted many of them. He came to respect most of the writers he satirized, and to become the personal friend of some, and two years after the poem's publication in 1809 he tried to prevent any further copies from being sold. But at least, when it first appeared, it proved that he was more than a sentimental schoolboy. And if sometimes he was cheap and thoughtless in the taunts he flung at his famous elders, he was only doing what high-spirited and angry young men have done throughout the history of literature.

The year 1808 was a full one for him, apart from the business of the *Edinburgh Review*.

That summer he took his degree at Cambridge—after some dispute with the university authorities, since he had been absent so much.

That summer, too, saw the end of Lord Grey's tenancy of Newstead. Byron took possession. The Abbey was still far from comfortable, but enough work had been done for Byron and his friends to live there in unconventional bachelor style. They rode and swam, got up late, played practical jokes, held parties far into the night, or went into Nottingham to attend fancy-dress balls and suchlike festivities. Byron loved dressing up. He liked Turkish and other picturesque Eastern costumes, but at Newstead itself the party would put on monks' robes because of what the house had once been. A human skull had been dug up in the gardens, and it tickled Byron's ghoulish fancy to have it made into a loving cup, so that it could be filled with wine and handed around. Gothic horror was a cult just then, favored by poets and novelists—Jane Austen pokes fun at them in *Northanger Abbey*—and Byron merely shared the general taste for ghost stories, skeletons, and romantic monastery ruins.

It was not surprising, though, that the household caused gossip in the district. It looked as if the behavior of the Wicked Lord was going to be matched by the strange antics of his successor. The tame bear, apt to alarm visitors with its embraces, was just one of the many oddities to be encountered there.

Byron loved animals and was continually adding to his collection of dogs. But his favorite was Boatswain, and that November the handsome Newfoundland went mad and died, "suffering much," wrote his heartbroken master, "yet retaining all the gentleness of his nature to the last, never attempting to do the least injury to any one near him."

The dog's elaborate tomb is still to be seen in the garden. Byron wrote a poem and also an epitaph, which runs:

> Near this spot
> Are deposited the Remains of one
> Who possessed Beauty without Vanity,
> Strength without Insolence,
> Courage without Ferocity,
> And all the Virtues of Man without his Vices.
> This Praise, which would be unmeaning Flattery
> If inscribed over human ashes,
> Is but a just tribute to the Memory of
> BOATSWAIN, a Dog,
> Who was born at Newfoundland, May, 1803,
> And died at Newstead Abbey, Nov. 18, 1808.

He was as fond as ever of his beautiful Nottinghamshire estate, but he was too young and restless to settle there as yet. Long before the end of his time at Cambridge he had been dreaming of a foreign journey he would make as soon as he was twenty-one.

For generations it had been the accepted custom for young English gentlemen to finish their education by making the Grand Tour, which involved a leisurely sightsee-

ing trip to Rome and Naples and back, taking in France
and Switzerland and possibly other countries on the way.
But in 1808 this was impossible, for Britain was at war
with France, and the French Emperor, Napoleon, held
most of Europe and the places usually visited.

Byron was not worried. He had no desire to travel the
track beaten by thousands of conventional tourists before
him. His interest lay in the lesser known countries of the
East—Turkey, Persia, and India. If he could get there, he
reckoned, he could travel quite cheaply, more cheaply indeed than he could live at home. His mother could give
up her own house at Southwell. She was welcome to live at
Newstead, so long as he was not there himself.

He began to write letters to influential people and to
find out if his journey was possible.

Meanwhile, in January, 1809, came his twenty-first
birthday.

For a young landowner, and especially a nobleman, this
should have been an occasion of great rejoicing. Indeed it
was so. The Newstead tenants and their work people arranged a proper program of celebrations. They were, said
Byron, "to have a good dinner and plenty of ale and
punch, and the rabble will have an ox and two sheep to
tear in pieces, with ale, and uproar." Only one thing was
missing to make the party go—the presence of the young
lord himself. With his usual disdain for convention, Byron
remained in London, refusing even Hanson's offer to put
on a dinner party in his honor, and dining quietly by himself on eggs, bacon, and a bottle of ale.

Now he was twenty-one he could claim his seat in the
House of Lords. He wrote to his guardian about it, hoping
that the Earl would offer to introduce him. But the Earl

was not well, and he had suffered in the past from this young man's apparent rudeness and indifference, so he did no more than send him details of the procedure.

This meant that Byron, without the Earl of Carlisle to speak for him, had to apply like an unknown stranger, proving who he was and what right he had to his title. It meant a great searching out of old documents. Byron found it tiresome, time-wasting, and humiliating. He was furious with his guardian—he had seen so little of him that he knew nothing of the nervous trouble from which the Earl was suffering. There was misunderstanding on both sides.

On March 13, the day fixed, a tense and white-faced young Byron entered the House of Lords, a solitary figure, not supported as was customary on such occasions by other peers. He advanced with his slightly limping gait to the table where an officer administered the oath. When this ceremony was completed, the Lord Chancellor rose from the woolsack, the traditional seat on which he presided over the meetings of the House, and put out his hand with a smile and a murmur of welcome. Once again, Byron's pride made him act stupidly. He was still boiling with indignation and was determined that nobody, even the Lord Chancellor, should patronize him. He touched the open hand only with his fingertips, bowed coldly, and turned away.

"I have taken my seat," he informed one of his friends, "and now I will go abroad."

⊱ 5 ⊰

"The World Is All
Before Me"

THE world is all before me," Byron wrote to his mother
from Falmouth, where the Lisbon packet lay becalmed in
the broad Cornish haven during the last week of June.

"I leave England without regret," he went on grandly,
adding dutifully (but perhaps not quite sincerely) that he
had no "wish to revisit any thing it contains, except *your-self*" and Newstead. If his financial position did not improve through the selling of his Rochdale estate—a tire-
some business which seemed to drag on endlessly—he
might take service with the Russians or Austrians, or "perhaps the Turkish, if I like their manners."

His mother was not to be alarmed if she did not hear
from him, though he promised to write from every port.
"The Continent is in a fine state," he reminded her.

That was true enough. But since Nelson's crushing victory at Trafalgar, the British held the sea. Britannia truly
"ruled the waves," and was to do so without serious chal-

lenge for the next hundred years. There was nothing to
stop Byron's sailing across the Mediterranean to Turkey,
then an empire covering Greece and most of the Balkan
peninsula, as well as what are now Syria, Israel, Iraq, and
other Middle Eastern states. On the way, he could visit
Portugal and southern Spain, where British forces were
holding off the French invaders, and the island of Malta,
which Napoleon had seized but had since lost to the British Navy.

Byron and his friend Hobhouse, who went with him
and made the practical arrangements, sensibly equipped
themselves with Army officers' uniforms. The scarlet coat
would be recognized and respected by friendly foreigners
everywhere. It would save them from being shot as spies if
they fell into enemy hands. That they had no right to
wear the uniform was a minor detail. They were not the
first British tourists to take such liberties.

Byron's valet, William Fletcher, packed fashionable ci-
vilian clothes as well. Even so, when they reached Gibraltar, his lordship paid a local tailor fifty guineas for "a most
superb uniform as a court dress, indispensable in travelling." It was indeed "indispensable" to make a good show,
for the traveler depended on letters of introduction and
the way he impressed officials, a situation not completely
unknown today.

Some English "milords," as they were called, took a pos-
itive retinue of servants. Byron and Hobhouse went almost simply. There was, besides Fletcher, old Joe Murray,
the Newstead butler. There was Robert Rushton, son of
one of the estate tenants, a youth for whom Byron felt
sympathy as "a friendless animal" like himself. Robert ap-
pears in the poem, *Childe Harold's Pilgrimage,* as a little

page, but in fact he was a fair boxer, and Byron used him as a sparring partner in his continual pursuit of physical fitness. The party was completed by a German servant named Friese, engaged because he had traveled in the East.

Childe Harold's Pilgrimage is a poetic version of this journey, cast in the elaborate verse form of the Spenserian stanza. "Childe" is archaic English for a young man of noble birth (the poem is full of such high-flown language), and it is not hard to guess the identity of "Harold."

> Whilome in Albion's isle there dwelt a youth,
> Who ne in Virtue's ways did take delight;
> But spent his days in riot most uncouth,
> And vexed with mirth the drowsy ear of Night.
> Ah me! in sooth he was a shameless wight,
> Sore given to revel, and ungodly glee;
> Few earthly things found favour in his sight
> Save concubines and carnal companie,
> And flaunting wassailers of high and low degree.

Newstead is unmistakably the "vast and venerable pile," there is a hint at the disappointing affair of Mary Chaworth, and the hero's own family is described:

> Childe Harold had a mother—not forgot,
> Though parting from that mother he did shun;
> A sister whom he loved, but saw her not
> Before his weary pilgrimage begun.

So, stanza by stanza, it is interesting to compare the poetic version of the journey (which Byron started to compose when they reached Albania a few months later) with the prosaic facts related in his letters home.

They sailed with about a dozen other passengers in the

Princess Elizabeth and made a quick passage of four and a half days to the Portuguese capital. The Bay of Biscay was fairly smooth. Even so, Byron admitted, "I have been seasick, and sick of the sea." But by the time he came to write his poem he had forgotten the worst of it.

> On, on the vessel flies, and land is gone,
> And winds are rude in Biscay's sleepless bay.
> Four days are sped, but with the fifth, anon,
> New shores descried make every bosom gay. . .

Lisbon looked splendid, rising on its hills from the broad river. When they landed, Byron and Hobhouse found it dirty and smelly, and its people quite literally lousy. The young men diverted themselves nonetheless, sightseeing, theater-going, and watching the local dancers. Byron insisted on swimming in the Tagus. He enjoyed talking to the monks in bad Latin, riding a mule and learning to swear at it in Portuguese, and eating too many oranges. He especially enjoyed an overnight excursion to Cintra, fifteen miles away, with its "palaces and gardens rising in the midst of rocks, cataracts, and precipices," as he told his mother and later depicted in verse:

> The horrid crags, by toppling convent crowned,
> The cork-trees hoar that clothe the shaggy steep. . .
> The torrents that from cliff to valley leap,
> The vine on high, the willow branch below. . .

These lush romantic landscapes delighted him. Only the poverty-stricken inhabitants were a disappointment—"Poor, paltry slaves! yet born 'midst noblest scenes—."

After two weeks the friends decided to go overland into southern Spain, taking only young Robert Rushton and a

Portuguese guide, while the rest of their party sailed on to Gibraltar with the heavy baggage. Crossing the Tagus by boat, they spent the night at an inn and set forth on hired horses the next morning at four o'clock.

It was quite an adventure they had planned, for their route lay through lonely cork forests and over high hills, in a land ravaged by war and likely to be so again. They passed "a vast number of crosses," indicating wayside murders. But Byron enjoyed the thrill of danger and was never without his pistols.

Their first objective was Seville, several hundred miles away. They crossed the frontier at the fortress town of Badajoz, and Byron could cry, with Childe Harold: "Oh, lovely Spain! renowned, romantic Land!" Badajoz had been the scene of recent fighting and was to see more bloodshed in the next three years before the British finally recovered it by storm and with terrible casualties.

Byron, though glad enough to wear a British officer's tunic, had no patriotic enthusiasm for the war against the French. He was critical of George III and the conservative policies of his own country. He was scornful of the kinglets and princelings Britain had taken as allies, petty tyrants like the King of Naples. Like many Americans of the time, he saw the progressive and constructive side of Napoleon's dreams for Europe, and had no wish to see the toppled governments put back on their pedestals as they were, five years later, after the Emperor's own overthrow.

So, in the stanzas describing Childe Harold's ride across the sierras, there are some lines which (however tiresome and obscure to the modern student) were highly topical and controversial when the poem was published: Byron's indignant reflections on the waste of human life in this

struggle among the European powers. Such passages were
to help in making the work so hotly discussed in London,
along with the vivid travel descriptions and the thinly disguised autobiographical interest.

Meanwhile, whatever the young man thought about war
and politics, there was exhilaration in those long days in
the saddle, crossing the mountains—"Oh! there is sweet-
ness in the mountain air / And Life. . ."—and descend-
ing to the "immense horizon-bounded plains" beyond.

"The horses are excellent," Byron wrote to a friend.
"We rode seventy miles a day. Eggs and wine, and hard
beds, are all the accommodation we found, and, in such
torrid weather, quite enough." It was late July, when the
heat and dust of Andalusia were at their worst, but he
went on, "My health is better than in England." There
was, indeed, nothing wrong with his health, but the exhaustion of late hours and irregular living sometimes
made him unduly concerned about it.

They took carriages for the last stage of their journey to
Seville, where they stayed for three days in very crowded
lodgings, the city being the temporary headquarters of the
free Spanish government which Britain was helping
against the French invaders. "A pleasant city," Byron
noted, "famous for oranges and women." He also admired
its cathedral.

They hired carriages again, two of them, drawn by four
horses each, for the next day's journey to Utrera. Then
they were back in the saddle once more. They rode to
Jerez, the wine center from which sherry takes its name,
and thence down to Puerto de Santa Maria, where a short
boat passage across the mouth of Cadiz Bay saved them a
lengthy and roundabout approach to the city. Byron was

charmed with "sweet Cadiz." They had a gay time there, visiting the theater, which they enjoyed, and a bullfight, which they did not, and Byron had the briefest of encounters (too brief to be reckoned even as a flirtation) with the beautiful and decidedly forthcoming daughter of a Spanish admiral. Reluctantly they continued their journey, sailing in a British frigate around the coast, past Cape Trafalgar, to rejoin their servants and baggage at Gibraltar.

There they stayed nearly two weeks. Byron was keen to make a trip across the Straits so that he could say he had set foot in Africa, but the wind was in the wrong quarter on the day he had planned the excursion. He had to satisfy himself with a distant view of Morocco. He and Hobhouse used to climb the Rock each evening to watch the sunset.

The next stage of their journey was by packet to Malta. They decided to take only the valet with them. Joe Murray was too old for the hardships that might lie ahead. Robert was too young. Byron wrote to Hanson, "Turkey is in too dangerous a state for boys to enter," and asked his mother to be kind to the youth. If anything happened to himself, there was provision for Robert in his will. They naturally paid off the Portuguese guide (who had been cheating them over the expenses) and came to the conclusion that, however useful Friese's knowledge of Persia might be if they ever got there, his company was a luxury they had better do without.

It was a leisurely voyage to Malta. They went ashore in Sardinia and Sicily, two other islands that the British command of the sea had kept safe from occupation by Napoleon. Sometimes their vessel was becalmed, and the captain took Byron in a boat to catch turtles. At other times they amused themselves with Byron's pistols, using empty bottles as targets, Byron the best marksman of them all. And as they sailed along the brown coastline of Sicily, with the honey-colored ruins of Greek temples rising from the cornfields, they gaily emptied some more bottles, toasting each other in the frothy champagne.

They stayed in Malta for three weeks. It was long enough for Byron to be captivated by a young English-woman, Mrs. Spencer Smith, the "fair Florence" mentioned in his poem. He was, he recalled in later years, "seized with an *everlasting* passion," but although they discussed running away together, the affair came to nothing. Byron and Hobhouse sailed on in a warship, *Spider*, with a convoy bound for Greece. Important tourists— lords and suchlike—took it as natural that the Royal Navy should help them on their way.

The two friends now entered the magic region in whose history and legends they had been steeped from childhood. Under the white arch of the brig's sail they saw "The isles of Greece, the isles of Greece! / Where burning Sappho loved and sung. . ."

They stared across the blue water at the shaggy cliffs of Ithaca, where Penelope had once waited for the return of Odysseus. They identified the narrow opening of the Ambracian Gulf, where Antony and Cleopatra's galleys had fled from the disastrous Battle of Actium. And on the very first day, at the entrance to the Gulf of Corinth, they saw in the distance a little town called Missolonghi, which was to play an unforeseeable part in Byron's future.

All this land, though still inhabited by Greeks, had been under the cruel and corrupt government of the

Turks for more than three centuries. The Turkish (or Ottoman) Empire had its capital at Constantinople, now Istanbul. Its European provinces included all Greece, Albania, much of modern Yugoslavia, and the rest of the Balkan peninsula. Napoleon's armies never pushed farther south than the Dalmatian coast, so that Byron and his companions could go ashore without fear of capture—at least by the French. Mountain brigands and wild Turkish soldiers were another matter.

In such circumstances Byron's keen sense of his own importance was an assset. He looked and behaved as these people expected an English "milord" to do. At each stage of his travels he used letters of introduction. British admirals and governors, Lord This and Sir That, British consuls, Turkish officials—all were pressed into service, and he took care that each one passed him on to the next with respectful recommendations. It was now that his splendid clothes and expensive English saddles proved their worth. Even the most ignorant Turk could see that here was a very eminent personage, and that there would be trouble if harm came to him. So, when Byron and Hobhouse started inland to visit Ali Pasha, the Turkish Governor, they were given two soldiers to escort them.

To reach Janina they made "a journey of three days over the mountains," Byron told his mother, "through a country of the most picturesque beauty." It was not an easy ride. They met with fierce rainstorms and sometimes had to stay in barracks. Luckily they had all their baggage with them, on spare horses, including their own bedsteads and bedding. Even so, Hobhouse grumbled that "properly speaking, the word comfort could not be applied to anything I ever saw out of England." Fletcher, the valet, was always complaining and hankering after the beef, beer, and wife he had left at home. George, the Greek guide they had engaged, was dishonest and overtalkative—but knew no Turkish.

Byron, however, reveled in the color and strangeness of it all. At last Janina lay before them, "houses, domes and minarets, glittering through gardens of orange and lemon trees, and from groves of cypresses—the lake spreading its smooth expanse at the foot of the city—the mountains rising abruptly from the banks. . ."

Ali Pasha was absent on a campaign, but had left orders that they were to be lodged in comfort and not allowed to pay for anything. After a pleasant week the travelers set out on another, even longer journey through the mountains to meet him at his country palace at Tepelene. Byron described to his mother the unforgettable scene when they arrived at sunset:

"The Albanians, in their dresses, (the most magnificent in the world, consisting of a long *white kilt,* gold-worked cloak, crimson velvet gold-laced jacket and waistcoat, silver-mounted pistols and daggers,) the Tartars with their high caps, the Turks in their vast pelisses and turbans, the soldiers and black slaves with the horses . . . two hundred steeds ready caparisoned to move in a moment, couriers entering or passing out with despatches, the kettle-drums beating. . ."

The next morning, to compete with this splendor, Byron called upon Ali Pasha in his "full suit of staff uniform, with a very magnificent sabre, etc." The Governor was a fat little man with a white beard and a kindly manner, which did not deceive Byron, who knew that he was really "a remorseless tyrant, guilty of the most horrible

cruelties, very brave" but also "barbarous." His first few
weeks in the country had been enough to open the young
poet's eyes to the true state of Greece under her Turkish
masters. But if one was to travel in the country at all,
it would have been madness not to accept the protection
of such a man.

After some weeks' travel in northern Greece, the Englishmen returned to the coast and embarked in one of
Ali's warships, which was to save them a long ride southwards. But the Turks were poor sailors—only the four
Greeks in the crew were real seamen—and when they ran
into a storm there was chaos. Sails split, cannon broke
from their fastenings and trundled dangerously across the
deck. The Turks called on Allah and went below, the captain in tears. George and his fellow Greeks prayed franti-
cally to the Saints. Fletcher bellowed about a "watery
grave" and never seeing his wife again. Byron, having
done his best to comfort him, wrapped himself in an Al-
banian cloak and went calmly to sleep. Somehow they
reached port in safety, and the Englishmen were thankful
to continue their journey by land.

The next few months were spent in Athens and other
parts of Greece. They saw the twin peaks of Parnassus,
home of the Muses, and Delphi, the dramatic gorge famous for its oracle. They stood on the battlefield where
once the Greeks had routed the Persian invaders.

They entered Athens on Christmas Day and found lodgings with a Mrs. Macri, widow of the British Vice-Consul.
Their rooms looked out upon a little yard with half a
dozen lemon trees. Mrs. Macri had three pretty daughters
in their teens. One, Theresa, dark and with a classical Gre-
cian nose, inspired his poem, "The Maid of Athens."

The city was then a dilapidated place with only ruins to recall its ancient glory. The Parthenon stood high on its crag, a pathetic, empty shell since the explosion, more than a century ago, when the Turks had used it to store gunpowder. Its splendid carvings had just been bought by Lord Elgin and were being packed for shipment to London, where they can still be viewed in the British Museum. Byron was disgusted at their removal, as some people are today, but if they had been left with the Turks, who cared nothing for such art, the marbles might not have survived at all.

In March the two friends sailed across the Aegean and visited Smyrna and Ephesus. Wherever they went, Hobhouse made copious notes and collected facts for the travel book he was planning. Byron made no notes but wandered about, eyes and ears open to impressions. He did, however, complete the second canto, or section, of *Childe Harold's Pilgrimage*.

They now embarked in a frigate bound for Constantinople. They were able to land and wander about the reputed site of Troy, which many scholars then dismissed as a fairy tale. In *Don Juan* Byron later wrote: "I've stood upon Achilles' tomb, / And heard Troy doubted! Time will doubt of Rome!" Sixty years later the German archaeologist Heinrich Schliemann's digging began to prove the reality of Troy.

Waiting for a favorable wind to take them through the narrow Dardanelles, Byron and a naval lieutenant imitated Leander's legendary swim across the Hellespont. The distance from Sestos in Europe to Abydos in Asia was not great, but the currents were strong, and Byron often boasted of this achievement.

At Constantinople they gave up the idea of going on to Persia. When they turned back, after several months' stay, Hobhouse went home to England. Byron spent another six months in Greece. He considered visiting Egypt, but the needful money did not arrive from Hanson, whose anxious letters advised him to sell Newstead. Byron doggedly refused. In November the faithful but grumbling Fletcher was sent home. Byron continued his solitary adventures, in Athens and elsewhere, until the spring.

Even he had by then had enough for the time being. He had endured malaria and other illnesses, but though his temper varied like his temperature, he was still the high-spirited and incorrigible young man who had set forth two years before. He had learned much. "If I am a poet," he once said, "the air of Greece has made me one."

He landed in England on July 14, 1811. He wrote kindly to his mother, promising to visit her as soon as he had completed necessary business in London. Reading his letter she said, "If I should be dead before he comes down, what a strange thing it would be!"

She was not well. He was asked to come to Newstead as soon as possible. On August 1, enraged by an upholsterer's bill, she had one of her hysterical attacks and died, without ever seeing her son again.

❧ 6 ❧

"Bad, Mad and Dangerous to Know"

BYRON's feelings on the death of his mother can be understood by every son and daughter who has ever raged impatiently against a tiresome parent and realized only too late the value of the bond between them.

Byron had often been embarrassed and irritated by his mother. He had avoided her company and her questions and her attempts to interfere. But at a safe distance he had loved her, and from far-off places he had sent her frequent and affectionate accounts of his travels. He had been bringing her back a shawl and some attar of roses, the costly Bulgarian perfume.

Even before the funeral he received another blow. His old Cambridge friend, Matthews, had been drowned that week. From the gloom of Newstead Byron wrote to Scrope Davies:

"Some curse hangs over me and mine. My mother lies a corpse in this house; one of my best friends is drowned in

a ditch. What can I say, or think, or do? I received a letter
from him the day before yesterday. My dear Scrope, if you
can spare a moment, do come down to me—I want a
friend. . . What will our poor Hobhouse feel? His letters
breathe but of Matthews."

On the night before his mother's funeral, a servant
found him sitting in the dark room beside her body. He
burst into tears and cried out: "I had but one friend in
the world, and she is gone." The next day, he could not
face the public ordeal of the ceremony. He watched the
procession leave the house with all the elaborate black
pomp that convention demanded. Then, turning indoors
and finding the faithful Robert Rushton at his elbow, he
told him to get the boxing gloves. For a few minutes they
sparred, Byron punching with far more violence than
usual. Suddenly he tore off the gloves and went away to his
room.

One consolation came out of those tragic days. He received a sympathetic letter from Augusta. There had been
a long silence between them. Now his half sister had a natural excuse to break down the barrier. The old, affectionate correspondence began again.

"I have not time to write half I have to say," she declared, "for my letter must go; but I prefer writing in a
hurry to not writing at all. You can't think how much I
feel for your grief and losses, or how much and constantly
I think of you lately. I began a letter to you in Town, but
destroyed it, from the fear of appearing troublesome. . . I
hope you won't think me a bore."

Augusta's marriage to Colonel Leigh was not going too
happily, and the Colonel, who was equerry to the Prince
of Wales, had quarreled with his illustrious master. Byron

assured her: "At all events, and in all situations, you have a brother in me, and a home here." He invited her to visit him at Newstead, where he was kept for much of that autumn, coping with estate affairs, but she was not able to come.

No one can mourn forever, least of all a young man of twenty-three, and Byron had numerous practical questions pressing on his mind and helping to distract him. "Peace be with the dead!" he wrote to R. C. Dallas, a distant relative who had arranged the publication of *English Bards* for him. "Regret cannot wake them . . . let us resume the dull business of life. . ."

Dallas rather fancied the role of literary agent to Byron, especially as the latter disdained the "dull business" of professional authorship and, though perpetually short of money, thought it beneath his dignity to earn it by writing. Dallas asked what he had written while abroad. Almost casually Bryon produced *Childe Harold's Pilgrimage* —and made Dallas a present of the copyright.

Dallas arranged for the poem to be published by John Murray, then established in Fleet Street, but soon to move to Albemarle Street, off Piccadilly, where this historic family publishing house still flourishes. Both Dallas and Murray, a shrewd businessman, saw the possibilities of the book, but they were nervous about some of the political and religious references that might give offense. Byron was begged to cut and alter. Mostly he refused. Dallas and other friends badgered him to read religious books and admit the truth of conventional beliefs. "I will read neither *pro* nor *con*," Byron retorted sharply. "God would have made His will known without books, considering how very few could read them when Jesus of Nazareth lived, had it been His pleasure to ratify any peculiar mode of worship."

And so 1811 passed into 1812, an eventful year in Byron's life and in the world generally—the year of Napoleon's disastrous retreat from Moscow, of Wellington's mounting success against the French armies in Spain, and of the United States' declaration of war on Britain. It was a brilliant year in London, with the Prince Regent now finally in control of the royal power, and the new whirling dance, the waltz, turning every ballroom into a scene of hectic gaiety.

In February Byron made his first speech in the House of Lords.

In the past months his own part of England, Nottinghamshire and the neighboring counties, had seen outbreaks of sabotage and violence committed under cover of darkness by bands of stocking makers and lace workers known as "Luddites," who broke the machines and burned the mills of unpopular employers. The whole region was like an occupied country, swarming with hussars and dragoons as well as magistrates and constables.

Byron was neither blind nor stupid. As he passed to and fro between the moldering magnificence of Newstead and the smartness of fashionable London he could not miss the signs of poverty or fail to realize that only appalling conditions had driven the workmen to such desperate actions. So, when the government brought in a bill to impose death as the penalty for machine-breaking, he stood up and spoke eloquently against it.

"I have been in some of the most oppressed provinces of Turkey," he declared, "but never under the most despotic of infidel governments did I behold such squalid wretchedness as I have seen since my return in the very heart of a Christian country. How can you carry the Bill into effect? Can you commit a whole country to their own prisons? Will you erect a gibbet in every field, and hang up men like scarecrows?"

It was a triumphant performance. The speech brought him many congratulations. He was appointed to a committee which reduced the death penalty to fine or imprisonment, but when the Bill went back to the House of Commons, the more savage punishment was restored.

By that time, however, London was talking not of Lord Byron's striking maiden speech, but of his astonishing poem.

Childe Harold's Pilgrimage burst upon the general public about a week after the House of Lords debate, but many advance copies had gone out to friends. One bore the inscription: "To Augusta, my dearest sister and my best friend, who has ever loved me much better than I deserved, this volume is presented by her father's son and most affectionate brother, B."

Some of the other advance copies, circulating quickly among influential people, prepared the ground for a runaway success, the minute the book went on sale in the shops.

It was, the Duchess of Devonshire wrote to her son, "on every table." The people were talking not of the war in Spain but of the new poet. "He is really the only topic almost of conversation." The book ran through seven editions in four weeks. "I awoke one morning," said Byron, "and found myself famous." Every one was wild to meet him. In St. James's Street, where he was staying, there was a traffic jam caused by the carriages driving up to deliver invitations.

Byron had never been exactly friendless before this—though he had an overdramatic habit of crying out that he was after each bereavement, whether it was an old college companion or his mother or even his dog who had died. Since his return from Greece he had made new friends, such as Thomas Moore, the Dublin grocer's son, still remembered for his smooth musical lyrics, *'T is the last rose of summer* and *Believe me, if all those endearing young charms,* and Thomas Campbell, who wrote patriotic poems beloved by earlier generations, *Ye Mariners of England* and *The Battle of the Baltic.* He had his old friends too, though Hobhouse (who has been called "the balance wheel in Byron's life") had joined the Army and was not always at hand when his good influence was most needed.

Friends like these—men friends, fellow writers, and others—offered laughter and ideas and argument at small dinner parties or in his publisher's drawing room. But the furore created by *Childe Harold* plunged him up to the neck in London's smartest society. "I was a lion," he recalled later, "a ball-room bard." He laughed at the fuss and loved it at the same time.

He was taken up by Beau Brummell and became a dandy; that June, he bought a dozen "fine white quilting waistcoats" and countless other elegant items. He was sought out by the Prince Regent at a reception, the Prince eager to meet the celebrated poet and holding him in talk for half an hour—for gross and impossible in some ways as the King's son was, he was genuinely interested in culture.

Certain great hostesses dominated London society—Lady Holland, Lady Melbourne, Lady Oxford, Lady Jersey—and they vied with one another to capture Byron for their parties. He spent more and more time at Holland House, a great curly-gabled Jacobean mansion in Kensington, and at Melbourne House in Whitehall.

It was at Melbourne House that he now met two young women destined to play a dramatic part in his life.

The first was Lady Caroline Lamb. An earl's daughter, two or three years older than Byron, she was married to William Lamb, son of Lord Melbourne. They lived in the upper part of the house and had a baby boy.

Caroline, however, was anything but a conventional young wife and mother. With her fair curls, dark hazel eyes, and boyish figure (she liked dressing up as a page), she was still very much the wild creature who in childhood had won nicknames like Ariel, Sprite, and Young Savage. She had never been tamed by formal education and was almost illiterate in her teens. Nonetheless, her impetuous temperament was matched by a quick enough intelligence. Later on, she was to produce several publishable novels.

She was lent *Childe Harold.* "I read it," she recalled, "and that was enough."

A friend warned her. "Byron has a club-foot and bites his nails."

"If he was as ugly as Aesop," she said, "I must know him."

Yet a few nights later at Lady Westmoreland's, when Byron stood there, ready to be introduced, she merely surveyed him with a long stare and turned on her heel without a word. In her private journal she entered her assessment of him: "Bad, mad and dangerous to know."

In fact, the danger lured her on. But she was not going

to compete with all the other women gushing over the
"ball-room bard." Snubbing him was the one sure way of
attracting his notice.

Their next encounter was at Lady Holland's. She was
visiting there when Byron was shown into the room. Her
hostess said: "May I present Lord Byron?" and the young
man tackled her directly. "That offer was made to you before. May I ask why you rejected it?" Whatever answer she
made, the matter was smoothed over. He asked if he might
call upon her at Melbourne House and did so the following day.

Thomas Moore and another of Byron's friends, the
banker-poet Samuel Rogers, were already there. "I was on
the sofa," she remembered afterwards. "I had just come in
from riding. I was filthy and heated. When Lord Byron
was announced, I flew out of the room to wash myself.
When I returned, Rogers said, 'Lord Byron, you are a
happy man. Lady Caroline has been sitting here in all her
dirt with us, but when you were announced, she flew to
beautify herself.' "

Now she wrote in her journal: "That beautiful pale
face is my fate." For the rest of that mad summer of 1812,
she behaved accordingly.

She was a young woman who could neither control nor
conceal her emotions. Even Byron, always ready for a fresh
love affair, had to beg her to behave more carefully. "Your
heart, my poor Caro (what a little volcano!)," he wrote,
"that pours *lava* through your veins; and yet I cannot wish
it a bit colder. . ." He thought her "the cleverest, most
agreeable, absurd, amiable, perplexing, dangerous, fascinating little being that lives." Love letters flew between
them. He was in and out of Melbourne House at all hours

and they were continually meeting at the same parties. That was not enough for Caroline. If he went to some function to which she was not herself invited, she would waylay him in the street outside. She would even appear at his lodgings in St. James's Street in some disguise, such as the scarlet and sepia livery of a Melbourne page.

It was too much, even for the aristocratic society of Regency England. Immorality was usually winked at, but the sinner was expected to keep up respectable appearances. Many married couples had not chosen each other originally: they had been pushed into marriage by their parents, anxious to combine family fortunes and estates. Once that was done, husbands and wives often went their own way, leaving Christian morality to the lower classes. But Caroline's insane behavior—and at times it was almost literally insane—created an open scandal. Even her easygoing husband, no saint himself, began to complain and talk of a legal separation.

Byron grew tired of her tantrums and the embarrassing scenes she made. He was thankful when, in September, her mother and husband carried her off to Ireland, out of the way, and he could turn to yet another of his short-lived love affairs.

He had not finished with "poor Caro." She pestered him with letters and, when she returned to London, demanded to see him. She forged a letter to obtain his portrait from John Murray. Byron began to refer to her as "that little maniac."

The scandal reached its height at a party in 1813. As he took Lady Rancliffe into the supper room, Caroline met him in the doorway and seized his hand. He felt a sharp knife against his skin. "I mean to use this," she whispered.

"Against me, I presume?" he answered in a low voice, and went on his way, hoping that no one had overheard.

There are different accounts of what happened a little while afterwards, and the most sensational stories appeared in the newspapers. Caroline was involved in some kind of scuffle, cut herself accidentally, and splashed her dress with blood. Byron did not know until later: her scuffle was with other people, who thought she intended suicide, and tried to disarm her. Whatever the truth, the public disgrace shocked even Caroline into some kind of shame. Her husband hustled her out of London and Byron for a time was troubled with her no more.

Very different was the second young woman he had met at Melbourne House. It happened on his very next visit there after Caroline's rush from the room to beautify herself.

Annabella Milbanke was a cousin of William Lamb's, very much a "country cousin" from the far north of England. She was sitting alone on a sofa in the crowded drawing room, so plainly dressed that Byron took her for a humble companion. In fact, she was a girl with rich prospects, but serious intellectual tastes, darkly beautiful, rather reserved, nineteen years old. She had been sent to London with a view to a suitable marriage.

They did not speak that first time, but each was aware of the other.

"She interested me exceedingly," Byron told a friend. He thought her piquant and pretty, and without the affectations of fashion.

Annabella wrote in her diary: "I should judge him sincere and independent." Though shocked by his reputation, she concluded that he was a good man led astray but capable of being saved. It was her tragedy that she soon began to see herself as the girl best qualified to reform him. "His poem," she explained to her mother, "sufficiently proves that he *can* feel nobly, but he has discouraged his own goodness."

As already recounted, Byron was fully occupied in the months that followed, discouraging his own goodness with Caroline Lamb. There was little room in his program for friendship with a thoughtful girl like Annabella, who had studied philosophy, mathematics, and classical literature.

She was, however, eventual heiress to a great fortune. To marry such an heiress was the accepted way to solve one's financial difficulties. Every one did it. His own father had done it twice. So, in October, when his tempestuous affair with Caroline had blown itself out, and a rich, respectable marriage seemed to offer a sensible solution to his problems, he actually proposed to Annabella—rather casually, and indirectly, through Lady Melbourne, her aunt, who also being Caroline's mother-in-law was only too anxious that this dangerous young man should settle down.

Not surprisingly, "the amiable Mathematician" (as he called Annabella) turned down this lukewarm proposal.

Byron wrote cheerfully to Lady Melbourne: "I thank you again for your efforts with my Princess of Parallelograms, who has puzzled you more than the Hypothenuse . . . we are two parallel lines prolonged to infinity side by side, but never to meet."

That autumn he was forced to put Newstead up for sale. There seemed no other course to take. It was sold, but in the end the buyer did not complete the deal. Byron was richer by the large deposit forfeited, but this money only staved off the evil day.

The year 1813 was as hectic as 1812, and still found him riding the crest of the wave. Somehow, despite successive love affairs and all the gaieties of London, he snatched time to write. He had a fluent pen and a colorful imagination. His poems were really popular novels in verse, full of excitement, passion, and horror, and he dashed them off as a clever thriller writer today produces a best-selling paperback. *The Giaour, The Bride of Abydos, The Corsair* (which sold 14,000 copies in a single day), and its sequel, *Lara,* entranced the public—but only with the last of these poems did he begin to accept money for himself.

"*Lara*," he admitted nonchalantly, "I wrote while undressing after coming home from balls and masquerades, in the year of revelry, 1814." *The Corsair* had taken him ten days, *The Bride* only four. He wore his success lightly and despised the public taste—but there were plenty of cultivated readers like Walter Scott who admired his work. The earnings, however, even from such sales and even when he kept them, were not on the scale of his reckless expenditure.

In June, 1813, he managed to meet Augusta. Improbable though it may sound, they had not seen each other—despite their warm letter-writing—since his departure abroad four years earlier. It was not of their choosing. "I have but one *relative*," he complained, "and her I never see. . . I wish you were not always buried in the bleak common near Newmarket." Augusta had now three little girls and a worthless husband who was usually away at race meetings.

When at last they were able to meet in London, Byron

and Augusta enjoyed themselves enormously. He took her to plays and parties, they laughed together and chattered endlessly, and he turned her shortened name, Gus, into Goose, not because she was stupid but because she gabbled. With her he could be entirely himself. There was the easiness of a brother-and-sister relationship, yet the excitement of exploring another personality, not spoiled by familiarity. He was having the best of both worlds.

She stayed in London for three weeks. Then he paid two visits to her home in Cambridgeshire, once bringing her back to London. He talked of going abroad again and of taking her with him. There was clearly something on his mind, and he hinted to friends of being "in a far more serious, and entirely new, scrape." Long afterwards it was to be said that the love between Byron and Augusta had burst the natural limits of brother-and-sister affection. It could be so, considering their passionate natures and the fact that they had grown up apart and met as any other young man and woman might have done. The truth is unlikely ever to be known beyond argument.

The idea of going abroad together came to nothing. But in January he took Augusta down to Newstead. It was an unusually hard winter, and, once their coach had struggled through to the Abbey, they were snowbound in the great house for weeks, unable to stir out and visit neighbors, but entirely happy in their own company. With bright coal blazing in his fireplaces and his cellar full of good wine, Byron was unusually relaxed. "Mrs. L. is with me," he wrote to Hanson, "and being in the family way renders it doubly necessary to remain till the roads are quite safe."

Augusta's child was born on April 15, and was named

Elizabeth Medora. Earlier that month, Byron went down
to stay with his half sister at her lonely Cambridgeshire
home—though her time was so near, Colonel Leigh had
not thought it necessary to stay with his wife, and was absent in Yorkshire. Was he in fact Medora's father? Or was
Byron? That possibility was publicly discussed only many
years after his death. It is still argued by scholars and no
absolute proof, one way or the other, can be established.

Certainly Byron seems to have loved Augusta more
truly than he ever loved any other woman. Unfortunately,
she was the one woman with whom he could not share his
life.

With whom, then? Augusta herself urged him to marry.
That summer they stayed together at the seaside. She
wanted him to propose to a friend of hers, Lady Charlotte
Leveson Gower. Byron had another idea.

For some time he had been corresponding with Annabella Milbanke. In itself, that meant nothing. In an age of
much leisure and no telephones, people like Byron scribbled hundreds of letters to friends and acquaintances. But
he found a certain interest in this intellectual girl—and
some day she would have money too.

In September, 1814, he proposed to her again. She said
"yes."

⚡ 7 ⚡

"The Treacle-Moon Is Over"

W E were married yesterday at ten upon the clock," Byron wrote to Lady Melbourne, addressing her now as "my dearest aunt." He was writing from Halnaby House, the Milbankes' family home at Darlington, which had been lent for the honeymoon. The bride sent her love, but was fast asleep on a corner of the sofa. "So there's an end of that matter," he continued, "and the beginning of many others. . . All those who are disposed to make presents may as well send them forthwith, and pray let them be handsome. . ."

The ceremony had taken place in the Milbankes' Seaham House on the Durham coast. Lady Milbanke had been "a little hysterical, and fine-feeling; and the kneeling was rather tedious, and the cushions hard; but upon the whole it did vastly well. The drawing-room at Seaham was the scene of our conjunction, and then we set off, according to approved custom, to be shut up by ourselves."

Byron's tone was deliberately light and unromantic. Indeed, there had been nothing romantic in his whole approach to the marriage, which had been practical. Between Annabella's acceptance and the actual ceremony there had been long weeks of discussion between the lawyers on both sides, planning the "settlements," or financial arrangements, a usual procedure in those days when brides' parents were alert to the risk of fortune-hunting bridegrooms. In the end, the marriage did not solve Byron's money problems. By a great effort he had managed for the moment to get his own income and expenses into some kind of balance, and he still planned to sell Newstead when he could find a buyer, so that he entered matrimony in a reasonably solvent state. Annabella's father, however, was heavily in debt, and, though she had a useful income of her own, she would not inherit her main fortune until her uncle and her mother died.

The lawyers concluded their talks. Byron obtained the marriage license. The wedding was planned for mid-December, a private ceremony, so there were no elaborate preparations to make. Even so, Byron dallied. He was perhaps the least impatient bridegroom on record. He decided to spend Christmas with Augusta. Then, taking only Hobhouse to support him, he set forth on the long northward drive. It was on January 2, 1815, that he knelt with Annabella on the hard cushions of the drawing room at Seaham House.

In a few weeks they were back there. "The treacle-moon is over," he wrote to Tom Moore, "and I am awake, and find myself married."

The visit was a bore. The coast was "dreary," though he

had clearly enjoyed seeing "the sea once more in all the glories of surf and foam—almost equal to the Bay of Biscay, and the interesting white squalls . . . of Archipelago memory." More and more, in the past year, his mind had been turning to foreign travel. Now, with the deposed Napoleon a prisoner on the Isle of Elba, Europe was at peace. When Byron's personal circumstances allowed, he meant to revisit the Mediterranean and see countries such as Italy that had been closed to him before.

Meanwhile, he was a bored bridegroom, staying with his tedious parents-in-law.

Sir Ralph Milbanke, he told Moore, had "recently made a speech at a Durham tax-meeting; and not only at Durham, but here, several times since after dinner. He is now, I believe, speaking it to himself (I left him in the middle) over various decanters, which can neither interrupt him nor fall asleep—as might possibly have been the case with some of his audience."

To Lady Melbourne he wrote in a less malicious vein, though he could not resist mentioning Sir Ralph's habit of repeating his public speeches over the private dinner table. "Bell," he emphasized, did *not* bore him. One wonders if this was still absolutely true. It is curious that he even thought of saying so, only one month after the wedding.

They were going to live in London, renting a house in the expensive Piccadilly Terrace, numbered, inauspiciously, thirteen. Byron wanted to visit Augusta by himself on the journey southwards. Bell, who had never met her new sister-in-law, since there had been no relatives at the wedding, not unreasonably insisted on going with him. Byron was in bad humor when they left Seaham House.

"Take care of Annabella," said Lady Milbanke. And as

their coach rumbled forward he turned to the girl and snarled: . . . "What on earth does your mother mean? I suppose you can take care of yourself?"

He was not always so unkind. His moods varied, but he was obviously under many stresses just then, and the visit to Augusta must have been sheer misery for Bell from beginning to end.

No one came out to welcome them when they arrived. They stood in the hall, Byron tearing open the letters that awaited him and scowling at one with troublesome business from Newstead. At last Augusta came hurry downstairs. She greeted Bell warmly. But she did not kiss her.

The Byrons stayed sixteen days. His bad moods continued. He teased both women with his cryptic remarks and often made Annabella feel that she was the unwanted outsider. At bedtime he would drop hints that she could go up alone, while he stayed downstairs talking to Augusta. He was unhappy and drank too much. When at last he tramped upstairs he could be heard swearing at Fletcher, who was still his valet. He hated sharing a bed. Once, Annabella recalled she must have drawn too close to him in her sleep, and he woke her with a furious "Don't touch me!" She cried herself to sleep again.

Their hostess did her best, but nobody, even Augusta could ever make Byron behave. During the daytime the little girls helped to ease the tension. They were, wrote Augusta, "delighted at being able to scream, 'Oh Byron!' again" and "approved much of their new aunt." After one of his pleasanter moods Annabella remarked to Augusta, as they discussed some of his portraits, "I should like to have him painted when he is looking at Medora."

His temper improved when they reached London and

moved into their new home in Piccadilly Terrace. "He was kinder than I had ever seen him," admitted Annabella. To outsiders the Byrons appeared a most devoted couple. At parties he was to be seen hanging over the back of her chair, introducing his friends to her, but otherwise scarcely talking to anyone else. When she went out for a drive, he saw her to the door with as much affection as if they were parting for a month.

If she had been jealous of Augusta at Newmarket, she normally managed to suppress the feeling. To some extent the two women were drawn together by their concern for Byron. More than once, that year, it was Annabella who invited Augusta to stay with them, heedless of his dark warning: "You are a fool for letting her come to the house, and you'll find it will make a great difference to *you* in all ways."

Soon it was evident that Annabella would have a child about the end of the year. "We have been very little out this season," Byron told Moore in June, "as I wish to keep her quiet in her present situation."

This thoughtfulness suited his own program, for he was busy with his literary friends and was never happier than with a group of keen-witted men. He described a typical evening with Sheridan, the hard-drinking playwright, and "others of note and notoriety." "Like other parties of the kind, it was first silent, then talky, then argumentative, then disputatious, then unintelligible, then altogethery, then inarticulate, and then drunk." At the finish, he and another man had to get the helpless author of *The School for Scandal* "down a damned corkscrew staircase" and deposit him safely at his house.

Byron was certainly drinking his share, and too much

for his own good, but he could be gay company without the help of alcohol. He had befriended the writer Leigh Hunt, just released from prison after his criticisms of the Prince Regent. Leigh Hunt's little boy had been given a magnificent rocking horse, and Byron would ride on it "with a childish glee."

Walter Scott found him "full of fun, frolic, wit, and whim . . . as playful as a kitten." The two men had met at last in April in the publisher's drawing room at 50 Albemarle Street. The younger John Murray long afterwards recalled those encounters.

Byron's "handsome countenance" was "remarkable for the fine blue veins which ran over his pale marble temples. He wore many rings on his fingers, and a brooch in his shirt-front, which was embroidered. When he called, he used to be dressed in a black dress coat . . . with grey, and sometimes nankeen trousers, his shirt open at the neck . . . He carried a stick. After Scott and he had ended their conversation in the drawing room, it was a curious sight to see the two greatest poets of the age—both lame—stumping downstairs side by side. They continued to meet in Albemarle Street every day, and remained together for two or three hours."

John Murray had just brought out Byron's latest volume of poems, *Hebrew Melodies*. It opened with: "She walks in beauty, like the night," a poem inspired not by any of Byron's loves but by a glimpse he had caught of a young cousin, Mrs. Wilmot, who was dressed in mourning but had enlivened the black with numerous spangles, suggesting the "starry skies" of the second line.

From being the rage of the ballroom, gushed over by sentimental ladies, Byron had advanced to something

more solid—a position of respect and influence in literary
London. It was not only Scott who admired him, though
disagreeing with him on political and religious questions.
Byron had long ago apologized to Scott in a letter for his
brash sneers in *English Bards*. It had been written, he said,
"when I was very young and very angry, and fully bent on
displaying my wrath and my wit; and now I am haunted
by the ghosts of my wholesale assertions." Since then, he
had similarly buried the hatchet with Coleridge and others he had once attacked. His reference to Coleridge, he
admitted, had been "pert, and petulant, and shallow
enough." No one could behave better than Byron—at
times—just as no one could behave worse, at others.

If he could be wild he could also be conscientious. That
year saw him in the unlikely role of committeeman. He
served on the subcommittee of management at the Theatre Royal in Drury Lane, then one of the only two li-
censed playhouses in London. It had just been rebuilt
after a fire and was going through difficulties. Byron cheerfully bore his share.

"The scenes I had to go through!" he wrote later. "The
authors, and the authoresses, and the milliners, and the
wild Irishmen—the people from Brighton, from Black-
wall, from Chatham, from Cheltenham, from Dublin,
from Dundee—who came in upon me! to all of whom it
was proper to give a civil answer and a hearing and a reading. . . Then the Committee! then the Sub-Committee!
we were but few, but never agreed. There was Peter
Moore who contradicted Kinnaird, and Kinnaird who contradicted everybody; then our two managers . . . and yet
we were all very zealous and in earnest to do good and so
forth."

It was the summer of Waterloo. Napoleon had escaped from Elba and landed in France on March 1. The Byrons' first gay months in London overlapped the historic "Hundred Days" during which the Emperor reoccupied his throne. Byron had never shared the patriotic British view of Napoleon, and he exclaimed with regret when he heard the news of his final defeat in Belgium. Wellington he respected, but for Napoleon's other adversaries he had only contempt. "Every hope of a republic is over," he lamented, "and we must go on under the old system. But I am sick at heart of politics and slaughters. . ." Hobhouse's brother, an Army captain, had been killed at Quatre-Bras, in the prelude to the main battle. "The havoc has not left a family out of its tender mercies."

The year wore on. The old money worries loomed up again. Newstead was still unsold. Annabella's rich uncle died, but as usual the immediate financial results were disappointing, and his estates went first to Annabella's mother, on condition that she and Sir Ralph changed their name to Noel. For Byron the bills still streamed in. He was threatened with the need to sell his books. A bailiff was actually sleeping in the house. John Murray heard of it, and immediately sent a large sum of money, promising more in a few weeks, to save the situation. Byron thanked him warmly, but was too proud to accept. He managed for the time being to retain his beloved library. Annabella's parents offered them the use of Seaham House, so that they could give up their expensive Piccadilly home. But even if Byron had been willing to retreat from London, his departure would probably have brought all his creditors down upon him immediately, like vultures.

By November he was becoming frantic with the worries

Catherine
Gordon, the
poet's mother.
*Courtesy of
John Murray*

Ada, Byron's
daughter. *The
Picture
Collection,
New York
Public Library*

Byron, age nineteen, with a friend. *Mansell*

Annabella
Milbanke,
the poet's wife.
*Nottingham
Public Libraries*

John Cam
Hobhouse,
"the balance
wheel in Byron's
life." *Mansell*

ABOVE: Newstead Priory, Byron's family home near Nottingham. *Nottingham Public Libraries.* BELOW: The hall of Trinity College, Cambridge. *Trinity College, Cambridge.*

Byron in 1813, the most sought-after celebrity in fashionable London. *National Portrait Gallery*

Byron in one of his favorite eastern costumes. *National Portrait Gallery*

Contessa Teresa
Guiccioli in
1818. *The
Picture
Collection,
New York
Public Library*

Caroline Lamb.
*Courtesy of
John Murray*

Mary Chaworth.
*The Picture
Collection,
New York
Public Library*

Claire
Clairmont.
*Nottingham
Public Libraries*

The Villa Diodati. *The Picture Collection, New York Public Library*

Cartoon of contemporary fashion; Bryon is on far left. *Mansell*

that pressed upon him. Outside his home he kept up appearances, masking his inner desperation behind the devil-may-care manner of a Regency dandy. But once inside the house he would break out in furious rages, torturing himself and Annabella—and Augusta too, when she stayed with them—by remarks of fiendish cruelty. Sometimes he would accuse Annabella of marrying him against his will and blame her for all his troubles. As soon as the child was born he would go abroad, "because a woman always loves her child better than her husband." He even taunted her with the threat that he would bring a young actress home and install her as his mistress. At other times he was all penitence. If they had met and married earlier, he said, she might have saved him. "It is too late now. But it is my destiny to ruin all I come near."

It is easy enough to see now that Byron and Annabella were the last couple in the world who should have married. It seems plain enough that Byron's appalling behavior in those weeks sprang from a combination of causes— money worries, incompatibility with his wife, the Byron family heritage of uncontrolled emotions, and the deeply buried remorse which he explained to no one. These causes also drove him to heavy drinking, which in turn intensified his brutality.

Annabella sought a simpler explanation. She thought her husband had literally gone mad. Even Augusta found it hard to contradict her. The two frightened women drew together to support each other, but there could never be complete understanding between them. "You don't know," said Augusta one evening, *"what* a fool I have been about him!"

On December 10, just after midday, Annabella gave

birth to a daughter. Byron seemed happy enough, though
Augusta believed he would have preferred a son. True, his
first remark was ambiguous as he smiled down at the baby:
"Oh, what an implement of torture have I acquired in
you!" The words might have meant anything or nothing
—that is the perpetual problem, how much value to give
to any isolated remark of Byron's—but many a new-made
father has said worse things in jest.

The little girl's names were registered as Augusta Ada,
and Augusta Leigh was to be one of the godmothers. But
when the actual christening took place nearly a year later,
different godmothers were chosen, and the child's first
name quietly dropped out of use.

Angry scenes continued between the young parents. To
every marriage, as to every quarrel, there are two sides.
Unfortunately, Byron's side has never been fully heard.
For what passed between the couple when they were alone
we have only Annabella's version, much of it poured out
in bitterness many years afterwards, when Byron was dead
and could not answer back.

It was decided that in the New Year the mother and
baby, as soon as they were fit to travel, should go down to
stay with Annabella's parents at their newly inherited
house in Leicestershire. Annabella spent her convales-
cence secretly trying to collect evidence that Byron was insane. She had his boxes and drawers turned out, his private papers examined. Behind his back, she consulted doctors and his own lawyer, Hanson. For the doctors she com-
piled a list of sixteen symptoms which, she considered,
showed that her husband was mentally deranged. But the
doctors would not commit themselves to a definite opinion.

On January 15, leaving her husband still asleep in his own room, Annabella went downstairs, stepped into the waiting carriage, and drove away with their child. A few days later Byron received an affectionate letter from her, announcing their safe arrival and inviting him to join them as soon as possible. She used their pet names, beginning "Dearest Duck" and ending, "Love to the good goose and everybody's love to you both from hence, Ever thy most loving Pippin . . . Pip . . . Ip." The "good goose" was, of course, Augusta.

Later, Annabella tried to justify this intimate tone. She had merely been following the doctors' advice, she said, and soothing a husband who had clearly gone out of his mind.

❧ 8 ❧

Exile

IT was in all senses a cruel winter. Deep frosts silvered London. The naked trees stood out spectrally in the hazy parks stretching away from Piccadilly.

Byron told friends he would soon be following his wife to Leicestershire. The trouble was, he said frankly, he could not stand her mother.

The dislike had become mutual. Lady Noel, as she was now called, was determined to deliver her daughter from this monster she had married. She spurred on the lawyers to contrive a legal separation. Letters were flying in all directions. Augusta, to her distress, was dragged into the consultations. She hinted that a separation might drive her half brother to suicide. "So much the better," said Lady Noel. "It is not fit such men should live."

On February 2 Byron received a letter from his father-in-law, announcing that both Annabella and her parents wanted a separation. He replied immediately. His own letter was calm, dignified, and sensible. He gave reasons why, in his present difficulties, it had seemed best for Annabella and the baby to leave London and why he himself had been compelled for the time being to remain. He had had a year of "distress without and disease within," and he could quote his doctor to explain that the latter had made him irritable. Annabella "may have seen me gloomy, and at times violent," but he denied "any particular ill-treatment." Of Annabella herself he wrote in the warmest terms.

What was the complaint against him? Annabella's father had made only a "vague and general" charge. Nor, in spite of repeated pleading, could Byron ever get his wife's family to say exactly what he was supposed to have done. Within a few days of his father-in-law's first letter, there was gossip about the separation all over London. Two of his best friends, Hobhouse and Lady Melbourne, warned him of the dark slanders being spread throughout society. More than a year later Byron was challenging his accusers to come into the open, say plainly what was in their minds, and test the matter in a court of law. But Annabella's parents and advisers said their lips were sealed. "If their lips are sealed up," said Byron, "they are not sealed up by me, and the greatest favour they can confer upon me will be to open them."

It was useless. Not only the drawing rooms but the newspapers buzzed with whispers of his unmentionable behavior. And, just because it *was* "unmentionable," neither Byron in his lifetime nor the most inquisitive students of the subject down to this day ever managed to establish clearly what the allegations were.

Byron did not give up his wife without a struggle. "Bell,

dearest Bell," he wrote, "I love you, bad or good, mad or rational, miserable or content, I love you, and shall do, to the dregs of my memory and existence."

She answered in cold, measured sentences. She admitted that she had been wrong in thinking he was mad. "I cannot attribute your 'state of mind,' " she wrote, "to any cause so much as the total dereliction of principle, which, since our marriage, you have professed and gloried in."

Byron could not move her. Nor could Augusta. Nor could Hobhouse or Hanson, whom Augusta rallied in support of her brother.

Poor Augusta had plenty on her mind just then. She was expecting another child. She had been honored by being appointed a lady in waiting to Queen Charlotte, and in the middle of March she took up her quarters in St. James's Palace. It was the worst possible moment for her to be caught up in the dark web of scandal overhanging Piccadilly Terrace a few hundred yards away. But, Byron said years afterwards, "she was, in the hour of need, as a tower of strength. Her affection was my last rallying point . . . Augusta knew all my weaknesses, but she had love enough to bear with them. . . She has given me such good advice, and yet, finding me incapable of following it, loved and pitied me but the more, because I was erring."

In *Don Juan*, two years after these events, he covered the old scars with a veil of cynical wit. The scene might be Seville, but the autobiographical element was obvious:

> Don José and the Donna Inez led
>   For some time an unhappy sort of life,
> Wishing each other, not divorced, but dead;
>   They lived respectably as man and wife,

Their conduct was exceedingly well-bred,
   And gave no outward signs of inward strife,
Until at length the smothered fire broke out,
And put the business past all kind of doubt.

For Inez called some druggists and physicians,
   And tried to prove her loving lord was *mad,*
But as he had some lucid intermissions,
   She next decided he was only *bad;*
Yet when they asked her for her depositions,
   No sort of explanation could be had,
Save that her duty both to man and God
Required this conduct—which seemed very odd.

She kept a journal, where his faults were noted,
   And opened certain trunks of books and letters,
All which might, if occasion served, be quoted. . .

And so the poem runs on, stanza after stanza matching the remembered reality, as if there were some painful ghost that could be exorcised with acid laughter.

Byron was hardly the best person to criticize the "very odd" conduct of others. But, it must be admitted in fairness, women did throw themselves at him, and, with the reflex of an experienced sportsman, he was apt to catch them almost automatically. That was why, amid the anguish of those weeks, there occurred his unsought, reluctant affair with Claire Clairmont.

One day in March he received a letter in an unknown feminine hand. "An utter stranger takes the liberty of addressing you. . ." Most authors are used to that kind of opening, but not, mercifully, to what followed: "If a

woman . . . should throw herself upon your mercy, if
with a beating heart she should confess the love she has
borne you many years . . . could you betray her, or would
you be silent as the grave?"

Byron sensibly ignored this effusion. His mysterious cor-
respondent then tried a more formal approach. "Lord
Byron is requested to state whether seven o'clock this Evening will be convenient to him to receive a lady to com-
municate with him on business of peculiar importance.
She desires to be admitted alone and with the utmost pri-
vacy."

Byron's easy good nature and a certain curiosity over-
came what little caution he possessed. Taking pen and
paper he replied: "Ld. B. is not aware of any 'importance' which can be attached by any person to an interview
with him, and more particularly by one with whom it does
not appear that he has the honour of being acquainted.
He will however be at home at the hour mentioned."

That evening, a Sunday, the girl called at 13 Piccadilly
Terrace. His first glance showed him that her alleged passion for him could scarcely date back "many years." She
was not eighteen. And she was not good-looking, though
she was striking in a dark, Italian way. She had the intense
manner that matched her determined assault upon him. It
soon appeared that she had an interesting and unconventional background.

She was the stepdaughter of William Godwin, a writer,
bookseller, and publisher notorious for his unorthodox
views on religion, marriage, and most other matters.
Claire—she was really "Mary Jane" but had adopted the
other name as more romantic—was living with her stepsister, Mary Godwin, and Mary's lover, a wild young poet of

twenty-three, who had already been expelled from Oxford, eloped with a schoolgirl, married her, and left her. His name was Shelley, Byron was interested to learn, for this must be the Shelley who had sent him a copy of his first book, *Queen Mab,* a rather crude and juvenile effort in which, nonetheless, Byron had found things to admire.

No doubt Claire's connection with Shelley made Byron more patient with her, for he did not find her physically attractive and he must have groaned inwardly when she asked his candid opinion on a novel she had half-written, containing a disguised attack on conventional morality. Few authors enjoy reading the unsolicited manuscripts of amateurs and Byron was prejudiced against intellectual women. However, he bore with Claire, they met again and exchanged letters, and he offered her (and Shelley) theater seats at Drury Lane.

Meanwhile the lawyers were drawing up the elaborate documents for his separation from Annabella, the custody of their child, and the future financial arrangements. As soon as the papers were signed, he was going to fulfill his long-delayed dream to travel abroad again. He was borrowing money for the journey. It was typical of him that, while the bailiffs were closing in upon his home, he ordered an expensive new coach to be built for him, modeled on one of Napoleon's and fitted with bookshelves and dining facilities.

His private life continued to be the favorite topic of the newspapers, which garnished it with every kind of scandalous guesswork. He still appeared in society, but it was not pleasant, especially for Augusta, who was cold-shouldered by many for her loyalty to him. People who had once crowded around them eagerly in ballroom and drawing

room now pointedly looked the other way. Yet he had his
supporters. He never forgot the gesture of Miss Mercer El-
phinstone, who was rich enough and redheaded enough to
care nothing for the docile herd. They were streaming out
of a room he had entered, as though suddenly conscious of
an unpleasant smell. This girl went up to him with a
friendly smile and said, "You should have married *me*,
and then this would not have happened to you!" He soon
afterwards sent her a grateful letter and a book he had
saved from his library, as a keepsake.

He had not finished with Claire Clairmont. It would be
truer to say that Claire had not finished with him. She had
grown up in the atmosphere of her stepfather's house,
with its constant talk of free love. She had accompanied
Mary Godwin and Shelley when they ran away together,
and since then, while Mary had been at a disadvantage,
bearing a child, she had contrived to switch Shelley's attention to herself. Under eighteen she might be, but
scarcely underexperienced. Now she brazenly wrote to
Byron:

"Have you then any objection to the following plan?
On Thursday evening we may go out of town together by
some stage or mail about the distance of ten or twelve
miles. There we shall be free and unknown; we can return
early the following morning."

Whether or not Byron accepted this invitation is not recorded. Certain it is, though, that somewhere, sometime,
during the final chaotic days in England, he gave way to
the girl who pestered him and whom he scarcely expected
to meet again.

On that point Claire had other views. Shelley also was
on the point of going abroad. Byron was making for Switz-

erland and was planning to stay in Geneva, where Hobhouse would join him as soon as he could get a passport—
Hobhouse was having some difficulty over this, as he had
been writing too favorably about Napoleon. What simpler, thought Claire, than to persuade Shelley to take his
own party via Geneva?

On April 21 Byron signed the deed of separation from
Annabella. Now he had nothing to keep him in England.
At crack of dawn on the twenty-third—early so as to escape the lurking bailiffs—he stepped into his new "Napo-
leonic" coach and set out for Dover.

He had said good-by to Augusta a week before, when
she left for Cambridgeshire. In the last flurried day of
packing he scribbled a note to her: "My own sweet Sis—
The deeds are signed—so that is over. All I have now to
beg or desire on the subject is—that you will never mention nor allude to Lady Byron's name again in any shape
—or on any occasion—except indispensable business."

He was only twenty-eight, but he had a feeling that he
would never see his sister again. He was right.

≫ 9 ≪

Summer by the Lake

A CROWD watched his dawn departure from Piccadilly, another crowd thronged around him on the quay when he embarked in the Ostend packet two days later, and soon the tourists in Switzerland would be training their telescopes upon him from a safe distance. He was notorious, a fascinating monster. The newspapers had made that clear.

Scrope Davies and Hobhouse drove with him to Dover and waved him off with promises to see him again soon. For the moment he had the company of Rushton and Fletcher, who had gone on his previous journey, a Swiss servant named Berger, and a young Italian doctor, Polidori.

Not only Byron but "Childe Harold" was off again. The continuation of that famous poem was fermenting in his mind. Again there was little attempt to hide the connection between fact and fiction. The new canto opened:

Is thy face like thy mother's, my fair child!
Ada! Sole daughter of my house and heart?
When last I saw thy young blue eyes they smiled,
And then we parted,—not as now we part,
But with a hope.

A few lines later came a reminiscence of the stormy crossing:

Once more upon the waters! Yet once more!
And the waves bound beneath me as a steed
That knows his rider. Welcome to their roar!
Swift be their guidance, wheresoe'er it lead!

In reality, the "wandering outlaw of his own dark mind" knew quite well where he was going. He was making for Venice. If, later on, he decided to go east again to Turkey, Venice would be a convenient port to sail from. Meanwhile he would take his leisurely way to Switzerland, and wait for Hobhouse and Davies to join him.

Belgium was dull. "Level roads don't suit me," he wrote to Augusta. "It must be either up hill or down. Imagine to yourself a succession of avenues with a Dutch spire at the end of each, and you see the road." He was bored by the art treasures of Antwerp, especially Rubens' paintings. "I never saw such an assemblage of florid nightmares," he told Hobhouse.

At Brussels he grew livelier. He was anxious to see the nearby battlefield of Waterloo. Though it was less than a year since Napoleon's defeat, the place was already a commercialized tourist attraction. Bullets, buttons, and other souvenirs were pressed on the visitor by eager vendors, and there were placards in English, announcing "to English and American Travellers" that coach excursions were

available daily at five francs, there and back. Byron visited
the spot with a Scottish major, a childhood acquaintance
he had run into in Brussels. He wanted to ride over the
battlefield before he left, so he and Polidori mounted
horses and went charging over the ground where so recently the French cuirassiers had galloped vainly against
the bristling bayonets of the British squares. That evening, the major's wife begged him to write some verses in
her album, and the next day he returned the book to her
with two of the famous stanzas on Waterloo, afterwards in-
corporated into *Childe Harold's Pilgrimage,* beginning:
"Stop!—for thy tread is on an Empire's dust!"

It was not the military details of the battle that interested him (though he listened politely to the major's ex-
planations), but the drama of Napoleon's downfall and the
tragic irony of the British officers' attendance at the Duchess of Richmond's ball in Brussels, only a few hours before
many of them were to be killed in action. This incident
inspired the familiar lines beginning: "There was a sound
of revelry by night. . ."

Claire Clairmont was meanwhile passing through Paris
on her way to Switzerland with the Shelleys. Strictly speaking, her stepsister was not yet "Mrs. Shelley." The young
poet's wife was still alive, but a few months later she was
found drowned in the Serpentine, the ornamental lake in
the middle of Hyde Park, and he became free to marry
Mary.

Byron's party had no passports for France, so they traveled at a leisurely pace up the Rhine Valley, keeping on
the German side of the frontier. The craggy scenery, the
racing water, the picturesque ruined castles, and the romantic legends were very much to Byron's taste and in

keeping with the new fashion for wildness and disorder which had superseded the eighteenth-century love of smooth, classical symmetry. "The castled Crag of Drachenfels / [he noted] Frowns o'er the wide and winding Rhine. . ."

High mountains, merely "horrid" to earlier generations, were now in vogue. Byron had genuinely loved them since his Scottish childhood, and soon, after passing into Switzerland by way of Basel, he was writing enthusiastically:

> Above me are the Alps,
> The Palaces of Nature, whose vast walls
> Have pinnacled in clouds their snowy scalps,
> And throned Eternity in icy halls
> Of cold Sublimity. . .

They drew near Geneva. They came down to the shores of the forty-five-mile long lake, pent crookedly between the Savoy Alps and the Jura Mountains, and known then more often as Lake Leman.

"Lake Leman woos me with its crystal face/ The mirror where the stars and mountains view. . ." Byron was soon to wish that only the lake had been there to woo him.

They stopped at Dejean's Hôtel d'Angleterre, just outside the town of Geneva. Byron was tired of answering officials' unnecessary questions and, when signing the register, entered his age as "100." When he woke up the next morning, his appetite for breakfast was not improved by receiving a note from Claire, who had been keeping a sharp eye on the register since arriving at the same hotel two weeks earlier.

"I am sorry you are grown so old," she wrote playfully,

"indeed I suspected you were 200, from the slowness of your journey. I suppose your venerable age could not bear quicker travelling. . ."

Byron put away the note, unanswered, ordered a carriage, and drove off with Polidori, house-hunting. It was then late May. He wanted a furnished villa for the summer, so that he could entertain Davies and Hobhouse when they came.

The house he eventually settled upon was the Villa Diodati, a square, gray house of stone with a tree-shaded courtyard and, running around three sides, a wrought-iron balcony with a superb view of the lake below. It was at Cologny, a short distance outside the city. Byron and Polidori took a boat for their first visit to inspect it. As they stepped ashore on their return, they walked straight into Shelley and the two girls.

Byron had already met Mary—Claire had made a point of bringing her to see him in London for a few minutes— and Mary had been enchanted by him. She was not yet nineteen, serenely beautiful, with hazel eyes, a broad forehead, and smooth, blond hair. She had now recovered her slender figure, following the birth of a son, William. Byron seems to have liked her well enough, but it was really the two poets, meeting for the first time in their lives, who took to each other at once and formed a strong friendship.

Four years younger than Byron, Shelley was tall with a slight stoop, bright blue eyes, and dark brown hair, worn long so that—with his pink-and-white complexion and delicate features—it gave him a deceptively girlish look. In fact, behind that sensitive appearance and excitable manner lay a basic toughness. Shelley had survived the ferocious bullying of Eton and the sadistic headmastership of Dr. Keate, who continually thrashed his pupils and once ended a sermon: "Now, boys, be pure in heart! For if not, I'll flog you until you are!" Oddly enough, Shelley *was* pure in heart, for all his views on free love and the disasters they helped to bring upon his circle. He was an idealist with principles, consistent to the point of being pigheaded. Byron was a cynic, speaking and acting according to his mood. They held for each other the attraction of opposites. At the same time there were similarities of situation that drew them together in common understanding —both poets, both just emerging from unhappy marriages and wearisome arguments with London lawyers, both fugitives to a foreign land where they could lick their wounds and start life anew.

Byron took the Villa Diodati. Shelley found another house nearer the water's edge, barely ten minutes' walk from Byron's through a vineyard. They joined together to buy a little sailing boat and kept it at a handy mooring close to the Shelleys' place.

That summer of 1816 was far from perfect, with rain, cloudy skies, and squalls, but, even so, the new friends enjoyed a good deal of sailing.

It is hard now to imagine the full beauty of the Swiss landscape as they saw it then. Sitting on his balcony, Byron could look across to an opposite shore on which only an occasional village peeped from the green foothills. There were no wholesale building developments, no unending streams of bright-painted cars, no express trains rattling between Geneva and Lausanne. And at night, in that age of candles indoors and coach lamps outside, there was nothing to diminish the brilliance of moon and stars reflected in the glassy water below or glimmering palely on the snowfields overhead.

There was silence, too, a silence almost unimaginable— to some people perhaps almost unendurable, today. Nothing to echo from the hills but the clop of hoofs, the bark of a dog, cow bells and church bells, a peasant singing—or perhaps Byron himself, breaking into the Tyrolese "Song of Liberty" as the boat sped before the breeze. "This quiet sail is as a noiseless wing," he wrote as he continued the third canto of *Childe Harold*.

On the cold, rainy evenings they would heap up a fire in the grand salon of Byron's villa and sit around it talking. They discussed every topic under the sun. Did ghosts exist? Would science one day make it possible to synthesize a living creature? Someone suggested a friendly contest: each should write a ghost story. Most of the efforts were left unfinished, but Mary Shelley, her imagination ablaze with their recent discussions, scribbled down a story that has never been forgotten. It was called *Frankenstein*. In this original version, Frankenstein was the name not of the monster but of its hapless inventor.

The general harmony of those weeks contained, for Byron, two discordant notes.

The first was the lovesick Claire, who had hung around him from the moment of his arrival, shamelessly writing to invite him secretly to her hotel room. Whether or not he accepted that invitation, he seems reluctantly to have renewed their brief London relationship when she reproached him for his cruel indifference. After all, he excused himself afterwards to Augusta, the girl "had scrambled eight hundred miles" to meet him. And, having been starved for affection recently, he "was fain to take a little love (if pressed particularly) by way of novelty." Claire's demands, however, were too much. Soon he was contriving never to be left alone with her. Claire had to express her devotion by making fair copies of his verses, but he insisted on her working at the Shelleys' house, not at the Villa Diodati.

The second, the less serious, discordancy lay in the character of the young doctor, Polidori—"Pollydolly," as Byron nicknamed him.

Byron's healthier way of life, now that he was away from his hard-drinking London set, made it unnecessary to have his own doctor on hand. Polidori became merely a paid companion, and an irritating one at that. On their way up the Rhine, he had been piqued by reading some warm praises of Byron's work, and had demanded: "What is there, pray, except writing poetry, that I cannot do better than you?"

"Three things," Byron had retorted. "First, I can hit the keyhole of that door with a pistol. Secondly, I can swim across that river. And thirdly, I can give you a damned good thrashing." The doctor had flung out of the room.

Polidori's presence became even less desirable after the meeting with Shelley. Offended because the younger poet had excelled him at sailing, the doctor challenged him to a duel. Shelley was no coward but he did not believe in duels, and he laughed at the idea. Byron, however, gave Polidori a plain warning. "Recollect," he said, "that though Shelley has some scruples about duelling, *I* have none—and shall be, at all times, ready to take his place."

Towards the end of June the two friends decided to take their boat on a thorough tour of the lake. Providentially the doctor had just sprained his ankle. They were able to leave him behind to entertain the girls and go off by themselves for ten days, with no companions save a couple of local boatmen, who did not intrude upon their conversation. "Thank God, Polidori is not here!" cried Byron, as they landed and explored "Clarens, sweet Clarens," which to young men of their generation and opinions was almost holy ground because of its associations with "the self-torturing sophist, wild Rousseau."

In all they spent an enjoyable ten days, coasting around the Lake of Geneva, and visiting places with historical and literary associations, such as the castle at Chillon, Vevey, where Rousseau had planned his *Julie, ou la Nouvelle Héloïse,* and the summerhouse in which Gibbon had finished *Decline and Fall.* The trip produced a whole poem, *The Prisoner of Chillon,* dashed off on two wet days, and some additional stanzas for *Childe Harold,* but it also very nearly put an end to two careers.

Early in the voyage their boat was caught in a sudden storm sweeping down from the end of the lake, raising high waves and churning the water to foam. Shelley could not swim. Byron saw that the boat was liable to turn over at any moment. Stripping off his own coat, he told Shelley to do the same and to take hold of an oar. He thought he could save him, he said, provided Shelley did not struggle. Shelley answered "with the greatest coolness" that Byron would have enough to do to save himself and was not to trouble about him. Fortunately for literature, their craft kept afloat and managed to run into the shelter of St. Gingolph.

Apart from that alarming episode, the trip had been a

delicious escape from care. Back at the villa, reality had to be faced again. Notably, in the person of Claire.

It was all very fine for Shelley to preach an idealistic free love, for Claire to despise the outworn conventions, and for Byron to run through a long series of casual affairs with any woman who invited him. But in that pre-scientific age, people who could not control their emotions could not control the consequences, either. Even the most temporary and superficial relationship, like Byron's with Claire the previous April, was apt to have a lasting result. Shelley now had to be told that Claire was pregnant.

What was to be done? Sensitive and kindhearted himself, Shelley was shocked by Byron's coarser and more callous attitude towards women. But his own experience had shown him that, even with the best of intentions, it was not easy to avoid hurting those one had loved. If Byron had been free to marry (which he was not, being only separated), it would clearly have been madness to tie himself to a second woman he did not love, having just painfully been parted from the first. Shelley came to the conclusion that the kindest policy, even from poor Claire's point of view, was to get her out of Byron's way and to take care of her in the months that lay ahead.

Byron, to do him justice, felt his responsibility for the unborn child. He suggested that Augusta would assume charge of it. When Claire refused, he offered to look after it himself from the age of twelve months—a singularly impracticable proposal from a man of his character and habits—but he was determined to have no more to do with Claire, who (he vowed) had only herself to blame.

The Shelleys were already planning to go back to Eng-

land. First, though, they went off on a short tour of Switzerland. Byron remained at the villa, writing, sailing by
himself, and when he wanted conversation, crossing the
water to Coppet, where Madame de Staël, a French writer
who seemed to have been everywhere and known everyone
of interest, provided a stimulating salon in her château.

The Shelleys came back for a few weeks, then started for
England at the end of August. Claire protested to the end
that she would love her "dearest dear Lord Byron" as long
as she lived. But any necessary message, after that, was included in his letters to Shelley. He never saw or wrote to
her again.

Byron's old Cambridge friends arrived just in time to
make Shelley's acquaintance. They had paused in Calais to
visit Scrope Davies' old gambling associate, Beau Brummell, whose immense debts had driven him abroad. It was
only three years before Davies himself had to flee to
Bruges for a similar reason, and he ended his days as an
expatriate in Paris, still drawing his stipend from the
Cambridge college that knew him no more. No two
friends of Byron presented a sharper contrast—Davies, the
spendthrift drunkard and dandy; Hobhouse, the conscientious traveler and writer, who later entered Parliament,
held office in the government, and ended his career as
Lord Broughton.

The trio got on together as happily as the Three Mus-
keteers, but it was perhaps just as well for Byron that Davies was the one who soon returned to England, while Hobhouse stayed to accompany him on the next stage of his
travels. Hobhouse wrote reassuringly to Augusta: "Your
excellent relative is living with the strictest attention to
decorum, and free from all offence, either to God, or man,

or woman. . . . A considerable change has taken place in his health; no brandy, no very late hours . . . neither passion nor perverseness. . . ."

Byron himself was writing to Augusta with the same affectionate frankness as ever. "We are the last persons in the world who ought—or could—cease to love one another." He was trying to get over the wreck of his marriage, but the separation, he said, "has broken my heart. I feel as if an elephant had trodden on it." But Augusta, though he did not realize it, was not so frank in reply. Lady Byron had been working on her feelings, applying a kind of moral blackmail, suggesting that, for Byron's own good, Augusta should have as little to do with him as possible. Miserable and bewildered, unequal to Annabella's logical and almost mathematical arguments, Augusta was browbeaten into obedience.

Davies had taken young Rushton back with him and Polidori's services were politely terminated. Thus it must have been with a sigh of relief that Byron set forth on a two-week tour of the mountains with Hobhouse, the companion of his earliest foreign travels. Fletcher continued as his valet, as indeed he did until the end.

Riding mules, the young friends explored the Bernese Oberland. They saw amazing glaciers, a waterfall nine hundred feet high, and "whole woods of withered pines" that reminded Byron of himself and his ill-fated family. They heard thunderous avalanches, "as if God was pelting the Devil down from Heaven with snow balls." They saw "the clouds foaming up from the valleys below us like the spray of the ocean of hell."

If these descriptions strike a modern reader as exaggerated, it should be remembered that Byron and Hobhouse

were being guided through a rugged, high-altitude world
which until a generation or two before had been unknown
and unappreciated, and which even then was visited by
only a trickle of sightseers. Mountain-climbing, skiing and
tobogganing, funicular railways, and mass tourism were
undreamed of. Once the traveler had mounted beyond the
last shepherd's hut, he was in a region of unaltered Nature, with dramatic scenic effects for which his eyes had
not been prepared even by a photograph, much less a mov-
ing picture.

Byron kept a journal of this tour—for Augusta's bene-
fit. "Dearest," he wrote, as he listened one evening to four
peasant girls singing folk songs he knew she would have
enjoyed, "you do not know how I should have liked this,
were you with me."

They returned to the Villa Diodati. They had seen
"some of the noblest views in the world." Now the summer
was over, and soon the Alpine passes would be blocked
with snow. It was time to be on their way to Venice.

Early in October their coach rumbled off along the lake-
side road and up the Rhone Valley. They had both admired Napoleon: now they could admire the magnificent
road his engineers had driven through the Simplon Pass.
Soon Lake Maggiore lay at their feet. They were in Italy.

❧ 10 ❦

"For the Sword Outwears
Its Sheath"

THE Italy Byron entered in 1816 was not the united country we know today. The long peninsula was a jigsaw puzzle of separate states. It had been so ever since the fall of the Roman Empire and it was to remain so for another half-century, until the time of Garibaldi.

Recently, when Napoleon had been rearranging Europe, there had been a brief Italian dream of liberation. Now, with Napoleon an exile on a mid-Atlantic islet, that dream had faded. The Italian people were parceled out again under half a dozen different masters: Spanish Bourbon royalty in the south, the Papal States slanting across the center, and most of the north—Lombardy and Venetia —ruled by an Austrian viceroy instructed from Vienna.

This was the region through which Byron and Hobhouse traveled to Venice.

They came first to Milan and stayed there several weeks, visiting the theaters and enjoying the social life of the city.

Byron was warmly welcomed as the most famous English poet then alive. People were much more interested in his work than in the scandals of his private life. The Italians were apt to shrug their shoulders over such matters. It was an accepted thing with them that girls married the husbands arranged for them by their families, and were afterwards free to carry on love affairs—with reasonable discretion—as they pleased. There was a regular phrase, *cavaliere servente,* "gentleman in attendance," to describe one who was acknowledged as a married woman's particular friend and escort on social occasions. If this was the free-and-easy attitude towards a wife's behavior, it may be imagined how tolerant Italian society was of a husband's, for it was a male-dominated society if ever there was one. This notion of the *cavaliere servente,* so odd to a modern mind, must be comprehended if upper-class life in Byron's Italy is to be understandable.

Certainly, nobody in Milan was shocked by gossip about this handsome young English milord who was in addition so brilliant a writer. Byron, however, was in no mood to take the offered opportunities for flirtations with the other sex. He was more ready to enjoy the conversation of the cultured men who thronged to meet him. It was fortunate that he had long ago studied Italian, though he spoke it, he admitted, "more fluently than accurately." But he was more at home in the language than in French, which he understood well but was shy of speaking.

Though Milan was an Italian city, the white-coated soldiers of Austria were everywhere, a continual reminder of the hated foreign power. Byron, who had always despised the reactionary monarchs of Europe, soon had a firsthand experience of the treatment served out to their subject peoples.

Polidori had reappeared in Milan, and Byron, with his usual easy good nature, welcomed him affably. One night, at the opera, an Austrian officer in a tall grenadier's hat planted himself in front of the doctor, completely blocking his view. Polidori asked him to take off his hat. The officer contemptuously refused and, after a few heated words had been exchanged—Polidori, as usual, inclined to be pompous and haughty himself—they both left the theater and went to the guard house. Word came to Byron, who was sitting in a box in another part of the theater, and he hurried out to the rescue. He found Polidori under arrest, but on presenting his card Byron was allowed to provide bail for him. The next morning the young doctor was served with a twenty-four-hour expulsion order from the Austrian dominions, and neither Byron nor the several Italian noblemen who interceded for him managed to get the order canceled. Byron's own name was filed by the secret police, and as time went by they became more and more suspicious of him.

Resuming their journey, Byron and Hobhouse crossed the wide plain of Lombardy, pausing at Verona to see the traditional but highly dubious tomb of Juliet, and arrived at Venice, in a gondola and in pouring rain, in the middle of November. Venice was far advanced in economic and political decay. The ancient republic had been finally overthrown by Napoleon and then assigned to the Austrian Emperor, so that citizens with proud memories of independence lived in the shadow of the detested black-and-yellow flag.

For all that, the city of canals and gondolas retained its visual magic. Byron was excited that at last he "stood in Venice, on the Bridge of Sighs." In the fourth and last canto of *Childe Harold* he wrote:

> I loved her from my boyhood; she to me
> Was as a fairy city of the heart,
> Rising like water-columns from the sea. . .

Yet he would not conceal from his distant English readers that the age of glory was over.

> In Venice Tasso's echoes are no more,
> And silent rows the songless gondolier;
> Her palaces are crumbling to the shore,
> And music meets not always now the ear:
> Those days are gone—but Beauty still is here.

After a week or two Hobhouse was joined by his brother and sister, and went off on a short tour with them, before returning to England. Except for his valet, Byron was now really alone.

After a year without love affairs (for he would scarcely have counted the embarrassing episode with Claire) he reverted to his old ways. He had found lodgings in the house of a draper and his beautiful young wife, and in less than a week he was writing to Thomas Moore: "I have fallen in love, which next to falling into the canal (which would be of no use as I can swim) is the best or worst thing I could do. . . Marianna is in her appearance like an antelope." He went on to describe her "large, black, oriental eyes," her clear, soft skin, her musical voice whether talking or singing, and her hair of the same "dark gloss, curl and colour" as Lady Jersey's. This "antelope" was easily caught: not many women could resist Byron.

Much of his time, however, he spent in very different company. He went daily to an Armenian monastery on one of the smaller islands in the lagoon and worked hard at, of all improbable subjects, the Armenian language. "I found," he told Moore, "that my mind wanted something craggy to break on." He got on well with the monks, who remembered him afterwards as "a quick young man, sociable, with burning eyes."

Mixed news came from England. Shelley wrote that Claire had given birth to a daughter, later called Allegra. John Murray wrote that the new volume of *Childe Harold* had repeated his previous success with the public, and so had *The Prisoner of Chillon*. At a booksellers' dinner the enterprising publisher had collected orders for seven thousand copies of each. This was gratifying. Byron was now accepting money for his poems, and though he did not, like most modern authors, get a royalty on the exact number of books sold, this success meant that Murray would be ready to pay a good sum for his future work.

Early in the New Year, Venice—and Byron—abandoned themselves to the annual carnival. In his poem he had exaggerated the "desolate cloud o'er Venice' lovely walls." In those carnival days the gondoliers were far from "songless," and the city throbbed with all its ancient gaiety, "The pleasant place of all festivity, / The Revel of the earth—the Masque of Italy!"

The celebrations were spread over a whole month. Byron had his box at the opera, went to masquerades and parties, and was seen everywhere at "conversatziones and various fooleries." He had always had tremendous vitality and enjoyed turning night into day, but even so the long program exhausted him. He confessed in a letter to

Moore: "I find 'the sword wearing out the scabbard,' though I have but just turned the corner of twenty-nine." He sent his friend a short poem expressing the same thought, perhaps one of the most haunting lyrics in the English language:

> So, we'll go no more a-roving
>   So late into the night,
> Though the heart be still as loving,
>   And the moon be still as bright.
>
> For the sword outwears its sheath,
>   And the soul outwears the breast,
> And the heart must pause to breathe,
>   And love itself have rest.
>
> Though the night was made for loving,
>   And the day returns too soon,
> Yet we'll go no more a-roving
>   By the light of the moon.

A bout of fever soon followed the exhaustion of the carnival. For several weeks he was seriously ill, and his recovery was not helped by an adverse criticism of his poetry in the *Edinburgh Review*. Though he might pose as indifferent, Byron was as much affected by wounding reviews as most authors are.

During his illness he must have done some hard thinking about himself and his future. He wrote again to Moore: "If I live ten years longer, you will see, however, that it is not over with me—I don't mean in literature for that is nothing; and it may seem odd to say, I do not think it is my vocation. But you will see that I shall do something or other—the times and fortune permitting. . . But I doubt whether my constitution will hold out." It was a prophetic letter.

When he was fit to travel he made a spring tour of several weeks to see Florence and Rome. He was anxious to avoid the crowds of English tourists, but not entirely successful. In Rome, on the roof of St. Peter's, he came face to face with Lady Liddell, a friend of his wife's family. Lady Liddell's party included her young daughter, Maria, and Byron's reputation seems to have been so diabolical, in those respectable circles, that the anxious mamma ordered the girl to keep her eyes down. "Don't look at him," she said, "he is dangerous to look at." If Maria was human enough to disobey the instruction, at least she seems to have suffered no harm, for in due course she married a marquis.

Byron for his part was more interested in looking at Rome and Florence. His impressions, and reflections, were joined with those on Venice to fill the last canto of *Childe Harold*. Here occur the lines on the Coliseum and the dying gladiator, which used to be made overfamiliar by the excessive enthusiasm of teachers, but which perhaps a modern reader can come upon, freshly, for himself. Here, too, as a contrast to ruins, tombs, and the Tiber's "marble wilderness," is the famous reminder that "There is a pleasure in the pathless woods, / There is a rapture on the lonely shore. . ."

At the end of May Byron returned to Venice. He had by no means made up his mind to stay abroad forever, but the puzzling tone of Augusta's letters did not encourage him—they seemed to have lost all their old frankness and spontaneity, as indeed they had. Augusta still loved her half brother, but was terrified lest he should reappear in England. The scandal of his marriage separation had shattered her. Annabella, with her stronger personality, had bullied her. Augusta had her own worries, with a worthless husband and a still-growing family—by 1820 the little Leighs numbered seven. She was not going to add to her troubles by pressing Byron to come home.

For the time being he was content where he was, or as content as it was in his restless nature ever to be.

> With all its sinful doings, I must say,
> That Italy's a pleasant place to me,
> Who love to see the Sun shine every day. . .

He declared this in a lighthearted poem, *Beppo,* which he wrote at this time, and which marks a new development in his style, away from the serious rhetorical tone of *Childe Harold* and towards the satirical conversational manner of *Don Juan.*

That autumn, 1817, Newstead was sold at last to one of his old schoolfellows at Harrow, and he was free from the money troubles that had plagued him ever since he could remember. He was able to pay off old debts, reassure Augusta that her husband would never have to refund a sum Byron had lent them in 1814 ("I would not take his money if he had it"), and live in the openhanded fashion that matched his character.

He now leased the Palazzo Mocenigo, an imposing gray mansion whose balconies hung over the Grand Canal and offered a sidelong glimpse of the Rialto Bridge. It had the customary private landing stage at the front door, and Byron's staff included a gondolier as well as a dozen other

Italians, among whom that typically John Bull English-man, Fletcher, must have felt sadly isolated.

It had been the practice for centuries for wealthy Vene-tians to have country houses on the mainland as well, and these villas, built in the elegant Palladian style, still line the shady banks of the River Brenta as it flows down to the lagoon from the direction of Padua. Byron rented one of these, the Villa Foscarini, about seven miles upriver at La Mira. The house itself was not one of the most attrac-tive, but it had a garden that the Italians imagined to be English-style, and it enabled Byron to enjoy rides in the neighborhood.

His four saddle horses became something of a legend in Venice, for he would not leave them at La Mira in the winter, but had them ferried over to the Lido, the long, narrow sand bar dividing the lagoon from the open sea. On what was then a solitary beach, alone or with some chosen friend like Hobhouse who came out to visit him, Byron would enjoy an afternoon gallop, returning to the city in his gondola as the wintry sun went down behind the incomparable Venetian skyline across the water.

"There are only eight horses in Venice," noted an Eng-lish visitor amusedly. "Four are of brass, over the gate of the cathedral, and the other four are alive in Lord Byron's stable."

Byron kept up his swimming too, not only from the Lido but in the Grand Canal itself, which would not ap-peal to many visitors today. In a contest with a friend, he once swam the whole width of the lagoon from the sand bar to the mouth of the Grand Canal, and won by five hundred yards.

In these Venetian years he slipped back into a life of dis-
sipation, with numerous love affairs in which there was little love, only sensual satisfaction. Often he would not get
up to breakfast until the early afternoon. Then, after long
evenings and nights of pleasure, he might sit writing until
dawn. Not only his letters, but some of his finest verses,
were written in the small hours.

He wrote as he lived, with a feverish, unhesitating
speed. He used playbills and any scrap of paper that came
to hand. His working methods were once described by the
Countess Guiccioli (pronounced *gwee*-cho-lee) who a year
or two later was to become the partner of his final love
affair.

"His pen moved so rapidly over the page," she recorded,
"that one day I said to him, 'One would almost believe
that someone was dictating to you!' 'Yes,' he replied, 'a
mischievous spirit who sometimes even makes me write
what I am not thinking.' "

The mischievous spirit was certainly conspicuous in the
poem he was now writing, *Don Juan,* a work spread, like
Childe Harold's Pilgrimage, over several years and published in various parts, but in its humorous colloquial
style much more akin to *Beppo.* From the beginning he
had fears lest it might be "too free for these very modest
days," and when John Murray received the first batch of
manuscript he agreed with Hobhouse, Scrope Davies, and
others that "it will be impossible to publish this." Byron,
however, stuck to his guns and refused nearly all the cuts
and changes demanded. Eventually he agreed that the first
edition should come out without a publisher's imprint
and without even the author's name to link the book with
Murray.

Byron might have been foreseeing this prudery when he described, in the first canto, his young hero's classical education:

> Juan was taught from out the best edition,
>   Expurgated by learnéd men, who place,
> Judiciously, from out the schoolboy's vision,
>   The grosser parts; but, fearful to deface
> Too much their modest bard by this omission,
>   And pitying sore his mutilated case,
> They only add them all in an appendix,
> Which saves, in fact, the trouble of an index.

Again Byron was writing a novel in verse, full of brilliant word-pictures of foreign scenes, interspersed with sly comments of his own and digs at eminent contemporary persons, from Wordsworth to the Duke of Wellington. His sixteen-year-old hero, after a strict upbringing in Seville, is led astray by a married woman, and sent abroad to keep him out of mischief. Juan is shipwrecked on a desert island and introduced to real love by Haidée, daughter of a Greek pirate. The subsequent cantos, written at intervals until 1823, take Juan to Constantinople as a slave and to St. Petersburg as a favorite of the Russian empress, Catherine the Great. The mood varies continually. Jokes and facetious rhymes give place to tender love scenes and evocative passages, such as the famous "Isles of Greece" stanzas. Add, finally, the obvious autobiographical elements—the merciless portrait of Annabella as Don Juan's learned and moral mother—and it may be imagined how the public rushed to buy the poem when the reluctant publisher put it on the market. Murray's house in Albemarle Street was besieged by booksellers' messengers. Parcels of copies had to be handed through the window to the impatient throng.

That was July, 1819. Before that, two events must be recorded. Byron's odd household had gained a new member: Claire's infant daughter, Allegra. The Shelleys were still looking after Claire but finding it difficult, in England, to explain the little girl's identity. It was agreed that Byron should do as he had always promised, and take over her upbringing. The Shelleys and Claire came out as far as Milan, but Byron was rock-like in his resolve never to meet the unfortunate young woman whom he blamed for the whole episode. A Swiss nurse, Elise, brought the child to him in Venice and remained to look after her. Byron was delighted with Allegra, an intelligent and attractive little girl with bright blue eyes. She was a compensation for the other daughter, Ada, whom his wife and the law courts prevented his ever seeing. Though Byron was the least domesticated of men, and probably one of the most unsuitable of parents, his complex nature included a proud and tender love for the children he had so irresponsibly helped to bring into the world. He welcomed Allegra. But the immoral atmospheres of the Palazzo Mocenigo and the Villa Foscarini were not the best in which to rear a child.

Allegra arrived at the end of April, 1818. A few months earlier Byron had spent the evening of his thirtieth birthday at a big private reception. There he had been introduced to an eighteen-year-old girl, petite, with rich auburn curls and liquid eyes, then glazed with weariness after a two-day journey from Ravenna, where she had just married a man three times her own age. The girl was too tired even to take in Byron's name. He, with his mind on other women at the time, soon forgot that he had even met her, though with automatic politeness he offered her his arm and took her over to look at a famous piece of sculpture.

The fatigued bride was the Countess Teresa Guiccioli. She was the woman destined to be, in Byron's own words, his "last passion."

≫ 11 ≪

The Last Passion

TERESA was the daughter of Count Ruggero Gamba, an Italian aristocrat with strong patriotic sympathies, who was involved with the Carbonari, an underground resistance movement plotting rather ineffectively against the various rulers of Italy. The Gambas belonged to Ravenna, a decayed little town in the Papal States, farther down the Adriatic coast. The proud capital of the Western Roman Empire in its last days, its harbor and canals had long silted up as the tideless sea withdrew and it was now a place of shadows and memories, dark pine woods and marshes, and glorious but neglected Byzantine churches.

Teresa went to school at a convent in Faenza, a few miles distant. There she learned to love the classical poets of her country, especially Dante, who was buried at Ravenna, and Petrarch, who had spent his later years only sixty or seventy miles away. When she was eighteen, her parents arranged for her to marry a local nobleman, Count Guiccioli.

Alessandro Guiccioli was then fifty-seven. He had been married twice before. His first wife had been much older than himself, but wealthy. For love he had turned to one of the housemaids, Angelica, who had borne him six illegitimate children. When his wife complained, he packed her off to an isolated villa and remained with Angelica in their Ravenna palazzo. Soon afterwards his wife died, leaving him all her riches—needless to say, there was gossip of poison—and the Count was free to wed Angelica. She in turn died in 1817, and the Count mastered his grief sufficiently to go to the theater the same evening. Having now all the wealth he needed, he could choose his next bride solely for her youth and charm. He accordingly arranged to visit his old friend, Count Gamba, and inspect Teresa. As the room was dark, and his sight not so good as it had been, he took up a candlestick and walked slowly around the girl, "as if," one of the family recalled afterwards, "he were engaged in buying a piece of furniture."

Count Gamba must have known more than enough about Count Guiccioli, but his enthusiasm for freedom was confined to the Italian struggle against the Austrians. The rights of women were quite another matter. This marriage to Count Guiccioli, who was so rich and who could hardly live forever, seemed to him a satisfactory way to provide for one of his daughters.

Teresa might be well-versed in literature, but, fresh from her convent, she knew little of life or even of her own nature. She had been brought up to obey the teachings of her religion and the wishes of her parents. She went meekly to the altar.

A year later she was beginning to mature as a young

woman and to yearn for something more than the narrow existence to which her marriage had condemned her. But it was not easy to assert herself in the face of Count Guiccioli's powerful will. Old he might be, but he still had a restless energy. He was passionately devoted to the theater (of which he was a generous patron), and he liked to go on to midnight parties afterwards. On the third evening of their honeymoon, they had no sooner reached Venice than he had hustled her off to a reception. Now, one April evening a year later, in 1819, when she was again tired and out of spirits, having just lost both her mother and her elder sister, the insensitive Count demanded that she should accompany him to the theater and then to Countess Benzoni's party. At the latter, he generously conceded, they need stay only five minutes. He had no one but himself to thank for the consequences.

It was nearly one o'clock in the morning when they reached the reception. The crowd was thinning, the candles burning down. Byron was sitting on a sofa with another Englishman. Countess Benzoni came across and asked him to meet the new arrivals. He begged to be excused.

"You know very well," he said, "that I do not want to make any new acquaintances with women. If they are ugly, because they are ugly. And if they are beautiful, because they are beautiful." It was an ungracious answer, but logical. He was reluctant to complicate his life with fresh involvements—and he was almost incapable of meeting women without an emotional reaction, one way or the other.

He gave way, however, to his hostess's insistence. He followed her across the salon and made his bow to Teresa. "Lord Byron," the older woman announced impressively, "peer of England—and its greatest poet!" Byron's somber expression—he deliberately cultivated a pose of tragic gloom—broke instantly into that extraordinarily charming smile which (said those who knew him well) so often conquered strangers at first meeting.

He and Teresa plunged into the usual small talk, but immediately it became something more. So, she came from Ravenna? He wanted to visit Ravenna to see the tomb of Dante. And because of the town's associations with the romantic love story of Francesca da Rimini. She was delighted to find the great English poet familiar with Italian literature. He, usually less interested in a girl's mind than in her face, was pleasantly surprised to find one well-equipped for the kind of conversation he enjoyed. They talked eagerly of their shared enthusiasms. She was amazed when her husband reappeared at her side, murmuring amusedly that the promised five minutes had long ago gone by. She rose to her feet, she remembered in later years, "as if coming out of a dream." She had "felt attracted to him by an irresistible force."

Byron had asked to see her again. They arranged to meet secretly, the very next day, while Count Guiccioli was taking his after-dinner nap. It was all highly romantic. An unknown gondolier called for her and ferried her to where Byron was waiting in his own craft. There were similar assignations by gondola each day after that. Teresa's excuse for these protracted voyagings was that she was studying French with the Guiccioli family governess, Fanny Silvestrini. Fanny served as the regular go-between

for the two lovers, as they became at their second rendez-
vous.

The idyll ended after ten days. Business recalled the
Guicciolis to Ravenna. But it was understood that Byron
would be visiting Ravenna shortly and would see them
again. He could hardly wait to view the burial place of
Dante.

"I am damnably in love," he wrote to Hobhouse, who
must have been getting used to such announcements. "She
is a sort of Italian Caroline Lamb, except that she is much
prettier, and not so savage. But she has the same red-hot
head, the same noble disdain of public opinion. . ."

She also reminded him of Augusta. "That turn for ridi-
cule," he later explained in a letter to his half sister, "like
Aunt Sophy and you and I and all the Byrons."

Caroline Lamb *and* Augusta . . . for Byron these re-
semblances made a powerful mixture. It almost seemed
that in Teresa he had found a girl for whom he could feel
not only physical passion but something deeper and more
lasting.

For the next month or two Teresa had to accompany the
Count on a tour of his various country estates. She and
Byron kept up a secret and fervent correspondence, but it
was not easy when she was traveling from place to place.
She became ill, and the doctor ordered her home to Ravenna. When, in June Byron made his projected visit to
the town and installed himself in a little hotel near Dante's
tomb, he was horrified to hear an exaggerated report that
the young Countess was "at death's door." The next evening, however, he was able to pay a social call upon her in
her sick room. Private conversation was of course impossi-

ble. He wrote to her in desperation: "You are so surrounded . . . I am writing to you in tears—and I am not a man who cries easily. When I cry my tears come from the heart, and are of blood."

Though Teresa's illness had been genuine enough, the separation from Byron—the first man she had really loved —had certainly made it worse, and she now showed a marked improvement. Soon she was able to get up, to go out in a carriage with him, finally to join him on horseback. They rode in Ravenna's famous *pineta,* the seaside forest of umbrella pines. "Everything on the earth," she remembered afterwards, "was green and fresh from the dews of the morning and the evening. The nightingales were singing. . ."

There was gossip about them. The Count ignored it. Teresa's brother, Pietro, was in Rome and there picked up the wilder legends of Byron's wickedness. He wrote to warn his sister. Byron, he had been told, had deserted a wife just as affectionate and innocent as herself. "He keeps her shut up in a castle," wrote Pietro, "of which many dark mysterious tales are told. It is even said that he has been a pirate during his journeys in the East."

Teresa remained blissfully in love. But her health was still delicate, and was not improved when her husband carried her off to Bologna, Byron following sociably in their wake. She decided she must go back to Venice to consult a doctor there. The Count was quite willing for Byron to escort her on the journey. The Venetian doctor prescribed country air. Byron hospitably offered the use of his villa at La Mira. The Count gratefully accepted for her. He had his own affairs to attend to. Also, in the troubled political condition of Italy, he hoped to use Byron's friendship to gain the protection of the British government, if ever revolution should break out.

Byron and Teresa passed the autumn at La Mira, which the young Countess considered an "earthly Paradise." Allegra, now nearly three years old, was there. The villa was large, and Byron, for the sake of appearances, lived officially in a separate wing.

Teresa was quite content to keep up "appearances" in the Italian manner, but Byron was not content to be her *cavaliere servente*. He would have preferred to carry her off openly, in the robust English style of an elopement. He talked sometimes of going to America. He still loved Italy, but chafed at the hypocritical conventions of its society. Perhaps he would go to Venezuela, taking Teresa and Allegra with him.

Teresa's father, like her brother, now became alarmed for her reputation. Count Gamba tried to make her give up this dangerous friendship. Then at last even Count Guiccioli decided it had gone too far. But when, after violent scenes with Teresa, he insisted on taking her home to Ravenna, the emotional girl made herself so ill that, in the end, Byron had to be invited there as the only remedy that would do her any good.

It was an impossible situation. Divorce, rare enough in England then, was unknown in Catholic Italy. Count Guiccioli could obtain only a separation. Teresa, the Church insisted, must live either with her father or in a convent. She preferred her father, who had swung around warmly in Byron's favor, and turned a blind eye on their relationship. For the next three years that relationship was as close to a settled marriage as the two lovers could make it.

Teresa's brother, Pietro, was also quite won over by the man against whom he had once warned her. Byron was drawn into the Gamba family circle and the plots they were weaving for the liberation of Italy. He let his own rooms be used for secret meetings and the storage of arms. He became the *capo,* or chief, of a contingent of would-be rebels, calling themselves the Cacciatori Americani, the "American Hunters." All liberals of the time looked to the United States as the home of freedom. It was the only great republic in a world of kings and emperors.

The revolution that Byron and the Gambas hoped for was to start in the southern Kingdom of Naples and spread from there. But the Neapolitan rebels were outwitted by their elderly King Ferdinand. He invited in the Austrian armies, always eager to repress any movement towards liberty. There were wholesale executions and public floggings. Other liberal sympathizers were thrown into dungeons or exiled to remote isles. A wave of tyrannical reaction washed over the other parts of Italy, and the pathetic, amateur revolutionary organization collapsed like a sand castle.

"All my friends exiled or arrested," Byron wrote from Ravenna to the British Consul-General in Venice. "The whole family of Gamba obliged to go to Florence. . ." Tuscany being a separate state, with a comparatively enlightened government, Florence attracted refugees from the rest of Italy.

The secret police hesitated to touch the famous English milord, but they now had a detailed file on his movements. "I can write but little," Byron explained to Moore, "as all letters are opened."

Teresa had had to go with her family. The alternative,

under the Pope's separation order, was to enter a nunnery. Byron stayed in Ravenna for some months longer, using all his influence to gain permission for the Gambas to return from exile. It was useless. Fortunately, just before the political crisis arose, Allegra had been sent to be educated at a convent, where the nuns adored her and she seemed to be happily settled. Byron wound up the rest of his affairs, and in October, 1821, set out for Tuscany.

His destination was not Florence but Pisa, the equally ancient city with the famous leaning tower. Pisa lay farther down the same River Arno, indeed almost on the western seacoast of Italy, and Teresa and the Gambas would join him there.

Shelley was there too, and had found him accommodations. The two poets were still firm friends, though Byron's unyielding harshness to Claire Clairmont caused the younger, gentler Englishman a good deal of pain. Shelley, however, had his own experience of Claire, and knew that she was no deceived innocent. He did what he could for her, and put her case to Byron as well as possible, but he was not going to ruin his friendship. He had now settled in Italy himself, and had more than once visited Byron, sharing his rides on the Lido and in the pine woods of Ravenna. Now, with Mary, he was furnishing a modest home on the upper floor of a house that faced the Arno.

His lordship, of course, had to have something more splendid—and, above all, more spacious. On his last visit to Byron, Shelley had been amused by the menagerie his friend had collected around him. The establishment, he wrote, "consists, besides servants, of ten horses, eight enormous dogs, three monkeys, five cats, an eagle, a crow, and a falcon," all except the horses roaming freely from room to room. He had no sooner listed them than he had to note also that he had "just met on the grand staircase five peacocks, two guinea hens, and an Egyptian crane." When Byron reached Pisa in procession with most of these, plus five carriages and six menservants, it was rather like a circus entering the town.

Shelley had found him a palazzo on the other side of the river. It was, Byron wrote to Murray, "large enough for a garrison, with dungeons below and cells in the walls, and so full of ghosts that the learned Fletcher (my valet) has begged leave to change his room, and then refused to occupy his new room, because there were more ghosts there than in the other."

Despite the friendly tone of this letter, Byron's relations with his publisher were becoming strained. Murray was increasingly alarmed by the poet's outspokenness in his later work, and asked for cuts and changes that Byron disdained to make. Byron called him "the most timid of God's booksellers" and took his poems elsewhere. But poor Murray wanted to keep in business, and out of prison, and Byron was a dangerous author to handle. When he followed up *Don Juan,* which had shocked so many, with *A Vision of Judgment,* which gave a ribald description of the recently dead King George III's arrival in Heaven, Murray must have been thankful that it was issued by another publisher, John Hunt, who was in fact prosecuted for his disrespect to the Royal Family.

Byron was happy. His relationship with Teresa had become calm and relaxed. The passion and the furtiveness were over, their connection was acknowledged everywhere. He had the Shelleys and other congenial English company.

Visitors arrived with the latest news from London. Teresa felt a little out of it at times, not knowing their language, but she made a friend of Mary Shelley, and the girls went on daily rides together.

One English visitor's presence was concealed from Byron. Claire came to stay with the Shelleys. She had a wild scheme to forge the necessary papers and snatch Allegra from her convent school near Ravenna. Shelley advised her not to pit her will against Byron's. For once it was perhaps unlucky that Claire did not follow her own instinct.

For soon afterwards, in April, 1822, Byron received news that Allegra had fever. He was greatly worried, though he hid his fears from everyone but Teresa. He sent word that the child was to have every attention. The doctor was not to leave her. If necessary, a specialist was to be fetched from Bologna. But within a few days a courier arrived, and Teresa had to break the news to Byron that his child was dead. He sat silent, stony-eyed with grief. Like all his affections, his feelings for Allegra had been fluctuating and inconsistent, but he certainly felt.

That summer the Shelleys took a house on the coast. Byron similarly rented a pink-walled mansion, the Villa Dupuy, just south of Leghorn, so that Teresa could enjoy the sea-bathing her doctor recommended. When they arrived, a squadron of American warships was paying a courtesy visit to the port. Byron went aboard and was delighted with the welcome given him by the officers. He told Moore that he would rather have "a nod from an American than a snuff-box from an emperor."

The two poets soon decided to take up sailing again, and recapture the pleasure of that earlier summer on the lake at Geneva. Shelley bought "a most beautiful boat," declaring with his usual enthusiasm that she "sailed like a witch." He named her *Ariel*. Byron was satisfied with nothing less than a schooner, built for him at Genoa, with a spacious cabin, velvet divans, marble baths, and a pair of small brass cannon bearing his coronet. He wanted to call her *Teresa,* but was persuaded that this might be indiscreet, so he named her *Bolivar,* after the South American revolutionary leader, which was almost equally shocking to the local Italian officials.

The friends were not destined to enjoy much sailing together. Late one night, when Byron and Teresa were staying at the palazzo in Pisa, there was a frantic knocking at the door. Soon Teresa's maid came upstairs, followed by Mary Shelley, looking "more like a ghost than a woman," and Jane Williams, wife of Shelley's sailing companion. Teresa met them, smiling. Mary stammered in English, "Where is he?" and then switched to Italian, *"Sapete alcuna cosa di Shelley?"* But neither Teresa nor Byron knew anything of him.

Mary explained that, some days before, Shelley and Williams had been at Leghorn, proposing to sail back to their wives at Lerici. The weather had been bad, and the women had not been surprised when several days passed without their arrival. They were thankful that their husbands had been too sensible to set out in such conditions. Then, to their horror, came a letter addressed to Shelley, which Mary opened and read: "Pray write to tell us how you got home, for they say that you had bad weather after you sailed Monday and we are anxious." The two wives started posthaste for Leghorn in the vain hope that it was a mistake, and that their husbands were still there. Passing

Byron's house at midnight, they called in to see if he had heard anything.

Byron's mind must have flashed back to the day of that squall on the lake in Switzerland. Once again he, who was so vain about his own skill as a swimmer, had lost one of his best friends by drowning.

Inquiries along the coast were organized by another of Shelley's circle, a Cornish ex-naval man named Trelawny, whom Byron had engaged to sail the *Bolivar* for him. After a week Shelley's body was washed up on the beach, horribly unrecognizable, but identified by a volume of Keats' poems that he had hurriedly thrust still open into his jacket pocket. It was little more than a year since Keats had died of tuberculosis in Rome at the age of twenty-five. Shelley himself had been just under thirty. It was an ill season for the young poets of England.

The health authorities had the bodies of Shelley and Williams buried in lime on the beaches where they had been found. The law forbade their exhumation for more decent burials elsewhere, but Trelawny was allowed to organize their burning, on great pyres of pine logs, and Byron was one of the few friends present at the strangely pagan ceremony. He cast a libation of wine and salt and frankincense upon the crackling flames. Then—responding to an impulse like that which had made him put on the boxing gloves on the day of his mother's funeral—he stripped and plunged into the sea, and struck out for his schooner, anchored a mile and a half offshore.

Shelley, he wrote to John Murray, "was without exception the best and least selfish man I ever knew." And to Tom Moore he wrote: "There is thus another man gone, about whom the world was ill-naturedly, and ignorantly, and brutally mistaken. It will, perhaps, do him justice *now*, when he can be no better for it."

Teresa's father, regarded as one of the most prominent liberal exiles, was now being hounded out of Tuscany: the government there was under pressure from the all-powerful Austrians to expel him. Shelley's death had in any case broken up the happy circle of friendship in Pisa. Without regret, therefore, Byron arranged to take Teresa and her family to Genoa, in the mainland territories of the King of Sardinia, the one corner of the country with a reasonably independent Italian government.

They left Pisa in September, 1822. Byron was in the final confusion of packing, "with hardly a stool to sit on," when to his surprise and delight Hobhouse arrived. They had not met since Venice, nearly five years before. Byron's eyes filled with tears. Unfortunately, Hobhouse could stay in Pisa only a few days, but in that time they rode together and talked of many things, especially political matters, for Hobhouse had been elected to Parliament. And they spoke of Greece, where the people had begun an armed struggle against their Turkish masters.

Hobhouse went off to Florence and Byron set out for Genoa with Teresa. He was never to see his old friend again.

At Genoa he rented the Casa Saluzzo, two miles outside the port, a tall palazzo with a splendid view over the bay. He worked on further sections of *Don Juan*. He wrote to Augusta, suggesting that she came out on a visit. She did not, but other British tourists appeared in Genoa to entertain him.

One was an old acquaintance, the Earl of Blessington,

touring with his beautiful young Irish Countess, famous
in London society as "the gorgeous Lady Blessington."
They stayed for a couple of months in Genoa, and Byron
spent a good deal of time with them, riding, sightseeing,
and attending the opera. Teresa could see that Byron had
something on his mind. Understandably—though as it
proved, quite unnecessarily—the Italian Countess devel-
oped jealous suspicions about the Irish.

The Blessingtons went on their way to the south. The
Earl, after much haggling, had bought the *Bolivar* but had
not managed to sell Byron a horse in return. After their
departure Byron continued to be preoccupied. But his
brooding had nothing to do with his recent visitors.

One day Teresa followed him into the garden. He told
her to leave him alone, then came after her, apologetic for
his apparent roughness. "How worried you look!" she exclaimed. "What is the matter?" He seemed about to say
something, but broke off as if he could not muster his
courage.

In the end it was her brother who prepared her for the
news. Pietro explained gently that Byron had asked him to
do so. For months Byron had been wrestling with his own
doubts, afraid to share his thoughts with her. Now, however, his mind was made up.

He was going to Greece, to fight for the liberation of the
country from the Turks.

≥ 12 ≤

"That Greece Might Still
Be Free"

TERESA heard the news as though it were a death sentence. She began by reproaching Byron, then demanded to go with him. But Greece, he pointed out, "was a precious place to go to at present." Certainly it was no place for a delicate young woman.

The Greek revolt had begun in April, 1821, a desperate attempt to throw off at last the Turkish yoke which had lain heavy on the country, and indeed on most of southeastern Europe, since the destruction of the Byzantine Empire in 1453. The Turks had answered the rebels with terrorism. They had taken the Patriarch Gregorios, the spiritual leader of all the Greek Christians in their empire, and hanged him in Constantinople in his sacred robes. In the following year they had sent troops to Chios, a large Greek island off the Asiatic coast, and had massacred twenty-five thousand people, carrying off another forty-five thousand into slavery.

The atrocities were not all on one side. The Greeks fought back with guerrilla methods. In many places the countryside was virtually taken over and the Turks were penned in the strongholds where they took refuge. One garrison was besieged on the Acropolis in Athens. The Greeks overwhelmed them and slaughtered them to a man —an act for which the Turkish army in due course took equally bloody vengeance.

In the western world, however, the public knew little of Greek savagery. Everyone knew that the Greeks were Christians, fighting Moslems. And the educated public, their minds filled with classical history and literature since childhood, saw the Greeks as the descendants of Homer, Plato, and the heroes of Thermopylae. A wave of sympathy swept over Britain. A committee was set up in London, on which Hobhouse was active, and funds were collected to help the rebels.

Byron, though far away, was elected to this committee. He was well known as a sympathizer. Had he not written as early as 1819 the famous lines in *Don Juan?*

> The mountains look on Marathon—
> And Marathon looks on the sea;
> And musing there an hour alone,
> I dream'd that Greece might still be free. . .

But, having known the modern Greeks at firsthand, he did not share all the rose-tinted illusions of the London committee. He had ordered, he wrote to Hobhouse, a quantity of gunpowder "and some hospital supplies to be sent up to the seat of the provisional Government. . . If I go there I shall do my best to civilize their mode of treating their prisoners." He would be much happier, he made it clear, if he could "only save a single life, whether Turk or Greek."

Luckily, at this time of agonizing indecision for Byron, Count Gamba was informed that he could return home from his exile—but he was expected to take his daughter with him. Byron could tell himself that he was not deserting Teresa. She would simply, for the time being, go back to Ravenna with her father. Her brother was determined to accompany Byron on his Greek adventure.

The war situation, in that summer of 1823, was very confused. Greece is all sea and mountains, which favored the rebels. The Greeks were better seamen than the Turks, who had always relied heavily on the former to man their ships. With so many Greeks in revolt, the Sultan had no sure hold on the sea communications so necessary to victory. Ashore, the rugged country lent itself to ambushes and other guerrilla tactics.

On the other hand, the very same geographical conditions had always made it hard for the Greeks to unite. In ancient times almost every island and every big mainland valley had formed a separate state in miniature. Local jealousies still embitter Greek politics today. So, in 1823, the rebels were split by rivalries and seemed unable to unite in one plan of operations against the enemy. Many behaved like pirates and brigands, and foreign well-wishers like Byron soon found their sympathy put under great strain. The full complexity of the problem did not reveal itself until he arrived there.

In the middle of July his affairs were settled and he was ready to leave. He had chartered a tub-like coal vessel for the voyage, with a rough old sea dog, Captain Scott, in command. Stalls had been fitted to take four of Byron's

horses and one of Trelawny's, and the *Bolivar*'s two small
cannon (strictly speaking, now Lord Blessington's property) had been coolly transferred to this other vessel,
named the *Hercules*. Arms and ammunition were loaded,
a year's medical stores for a thousand men, and a good
deal of money in cash and letters of credit. Nor had Byron
forgotten uniforms. He had provided himself with a ward-
robe of military magnificence. For Pietro he ordered a
green shako with a figure of Athene, while for himself and
Trelawny (who rather made fun of them) he commis-
sioned two gilded helmets with towering plumes that
Achilles and Ajax would have been proud to wear. Byron
was still the same old mixture of sentimental poseur and
cynical realist. Into this Noah's Ark he packed his bulldog,
Moretto, and his mountainous Newfoundland, Lyon, together with his Venetian gondolier, Trelawny's black
American servant, a young doctor, and a variety of other
attendants, including, needless to say, the ever-faithful,
ever-grumbling Fletcher.

On July 13 "the fatal day arrived," as Teresa wrote de-
spairingly. Byron had to leave the Casa Saluzzo at five. He
spent the last afternoon alone with her, and had thought-
fully arranged for Mary Shelley to arrive as he left, so that
Teresa should not be without company. The actual sailing
of the *Hercules* was rather an anticlimax. The weather
was so calm that they could only put to sea by the courtesy
of some American vessels which lowered boats to give the
Hercules a tow. Then, overnight, such a storm arose that
she was driven back to her former anchorage. By this time
Teresa was well on the road to Ravenna, and the couple
were spared the misery of a second parting.

From Leghorn Byron sent a hasty note in English,

which she had begun to learn: "My dearest Teresa—I have but a few moments to say that we are all well. . . Believe that I always *love* you—and that a thousand words could only express the same idea—ever dearest yours. . ."

The *Hercules* coasted down the west of Italy, through the Straits of Messina, and into the Ionian Sea. The Ionian Islands had been under British protection since Napoleon's defeat, and Byron made for one of them, Cephalonia, where the British Resident was known for his sympathy with the Greek rebels. Here the party could wait safely under the shelter of the Union Jack, unmolested by the Turks, until they knew better how the situation was developing on the mainland.

Cephalonia lay opposite the entrance to the Gulf of Corinth. On the northern side of the Gulf, at Missolonghi, the provisional government representing the main section of the rebels had set up its capital and driven back a Turkish attack. This government, under Prince Mavrocordatos, was trying to convince Byron that it was the authority he should deal with—but so were various rival groups. Byron was disgusted with these intrigues. "I did not come here to join a faction, but a nation," he said. He was impatient to get down to the real struggle against the Turks, but he knew he must go cautiously, or his munitions, funds, and the propaganda value of his name might be used to support the wrong party.

That autumn, while he waited impatiently at Cephalonia, he visited the next island, Ithaca, the legendary home of Odysseus. Someone suggested that he might like to see the places mentioned in Homer.

"Do I look like one of those emasculated fogies?" he retorted. "Let's have a swim. I hate antiquarian twaddle. Do people think I have no lucid intervals, that I come to Greece to scribble more nonsense? I will show them that I can do something better. I wish I had never written a line, to have it cast in my teeth at every turn."

Always, inside the poet, there was a man of action struggling to get out. What had he written, years before, to Tom Moore? "If I live ten years longer, you will see. . . I shall do something or other . . . I don't mean in literature for that is nothing. . ."

Just after Christmas he sailed for Missolonghi, narrowly escaping shipwreck and capture by a Turkish warship. On arrival he was hailed, Pietro Gamba told his sister, "like a delivering angel." He brought money for the penniless soldiers, munitions for their struggle, and the magic of a name famous throughout Europe. In Greece that name keeps its magic still. The English milord has never been forgotten.

For all his plumed helmet and play-acting, Byron showed in those early months of 1824 that he possessed solid abilities. He had to use infinite tact and patience, qualities which never came easily to him but were essential in handling the Greeks. The London committee, of which he was the representative, had little idea of the problems to be coped with on the spot.

If there was one uninspiring corner of Greece, that land of soaring peaks and glittering seas, of wine-like air and brilliant light, it was surely the poverty-stricken town of Missolonghi, a few hundred houses surrounded by stagnant malarial lagoons and marshes. The building in which the "delivering angel" had to take up his abode was itself damp, cheerless, and in that winter weather approachable only across a sea of mud. The lower half was occupied by a Colonel Stanhope, one of the other foreign volunteers, British, German, and others, who had come to help the Greeks. Byron had a bedroom and living room upstairs, sparsely furnished, redeemed only by a superb view of the mountains on the southern side of the gulf. Fletcher made him as comfortable as possible, and Trelawny's black servant, now working for Byron, cooked expertly and also groomed his horses.

Byron's birthday fell a week or two after his arrival. He was only thirty-six, but he had already packed so much into his life that he felt much older. His health troubled him. There had been some doubt, back in Genoa, whether he was fit for this adventure. "If I live ten years longer," he had written in that letter to Moore in 1817, adding ominously, "But I doubt whether my constitution will hold out."

That January morning in 1824 he came out of his bedroom and greeted Colonel Stanhope with a smile. "You were complaining the other day that I never write any poetry now—this is my birthday, and I have just finished something which, I think, is better than I usually write." Literary critics may quibble about that judgment, but there will always be a poignancy in the verses he headed, *"On This Day I Complete My Thirty-sixth Year."* They run, in part:

> My days are in the yellow leaf;
>> The flowers and fruits of Love are gone;
> The worm, the canker and the grief
>> Are mine alone!

If thou regret'st thy youth, *why live?*
The land of honourable death
Is here:—up to the field, and give
Away thy breath!

Seek out—less often sought than found—
A soldier's grave, for thee the best;
Then look around, and choose thy ground,
And take thy rest.

He had never been afraid of death. Now it almost
seemed that he wanted it. A premonition hung over him.
Perhaps his own body was sending him warning signals.
Perhaps he was anxious not to end his career with some ig-
noble disease. To his theatrical nature and sense of style it
was far preferable to find a hero's death amid cannon
smoke and flashing sabers.

So, in his discussions with the Greek leaders, he urged
them to take bold action. As a first step, let them attack
the Turkish fort at Lepanto, farther up the northern
shore of the gulf. To do this, they must have artillery.
Byron set about forming an artillery unit. He was also
commander of six hundred infantrymen—picturesque cut-
throats wearing the brief white kilt, or *fustanella,* that is
still ceremonial dress in some Greek regiments. A body-
guard of these men slept in the outhouses, and he used to
drill them in the courtyard. He was promised that, if the
campaign took place, his command might be increased to
three thousand. The Greeks were so jealous of each other
that they would agree more willingly to take orders from a
famous foreigner. What was no less to the point, the English milord had money to pay them. No one else had.

Riots and mutinies flared up and Byron had to settle

them as best he could. He was becoming disillusioned about the situation, but he never despaired. He applied his mind to the practical problems. He tried to instill some discipline and get some military training under way. He opened a public dispensary to attend the sick. He exerted himself to protect Turkish women and children refugees from ill treatment and even murder. Though he was impatient of paper work and formalities, he was clear-headed and decisive in dealing with vital questions. The energy he had once thrown into the business of the Drury Lane Theatre he now devoted to the muddle at Missolonghi.

He wrote only briefly to Teresa, but cheerfully. Perhaps in the spring she could come across to Zante, one of the British-protected Ionian Islands, and they could meet there. Did he expect that reunion ever to take place? Or was he merely trying to keep her happy?

It is no exaggeration to say that the shadow of death was already stealing over him. As early as February he suffered some violent seizure, which may have been a stroke. On the morning of April 9 he was delighted to get a letter from Augusta. It enclosed a black paper silhouette of Ada, the child he had not seen since just after her birth, eight years before. He relied on his sister to keep him informed. Annabella did not correspond with him, but she had recently written out a description of the little girl's character and activities, and given it to Augusta to forward. Byron took a pathetic interest in the daughter he was not allowed to meet, and he set off for his ride that morning in a cheerful mood. Soon afterwards there was a thunderstorm, and he was drenched to the skin before he could get back. This led to the chill and fever of his last illness.

But it was more than fever. His health had been deteriorating steadily. Modern medical experts have puzzled over the descriptions of his symptoms and treatment, and the account of the post-mortem examination later carried out by the cluster of doctors—British, German, and Greek —who surrounded him. Byron had little faith in them, or their favorite remedy, which was to bleed the patient. He swore at them, called them a "set of butchers," and resisted them while he had strength, but in the end they had their way, and drew off quantities of his blood.

For a week he still managed to deal with business and give orders, struggling out of his bed to do so. Then he began to have spells of delirium. He shouted in English and Italian. He imagined he was leading his troops against the Turks. "Forward!" he cried. "Forward! Courage! Don't be afraid! Follow my example!" In lucid moments he gave Fletcher his last wishes. He became incoherent again, exclaiming: "My wife—my child—Ada—my poor sister—go and tell my sister—go to Hobhouse—tell Hobhouse—"

On the evening of April 18 he murmured quietly, "I want to sleep now," and passed into unconsciousness. He did not wake again. Just twenty-four hours later the restless heart found rest at last. That same evening, with an appropriateness Byron himself would have appreciated, another terrific thunderstorm broke over Missolonghi. The noise rolled from mountain to mountain. Incessant lightning played on the waters of the gulf. And huddled in their cottages the superstitious Greeks took it as a sign, crossed themselves, and told each other, "The great man is gone!"

In his last days Byron had known he was dying. He had come to Greece, he made it clear, with the deliberate intention of giving his life for that country's liberation. "Here let my bones moulder," he begged. "Lay me in the first corner without pomp or nonsense."

As often happens with last wishes, all Byron's requests were disregarded.

His body—which he had always kept fiercely private, because of his deformed foot—was subjected to a post-mortem examination, embalmed, and sent by ship to England. On the morrow of his death the guns of Missolonghi boomed at slow intervals in melancholy salute and, as the news percolated through Greece, memorial services were held everywhere in his honor.

Nor did the "pomp or nonsense" diminish when the body reached England. John Murray tried to arrange for the supreme national honor of burial, with so many other poets, in Westminster Abbey, but the Dean refused permission because of Byron's scandalous reputation. For some days the coffin lay in state at a house close by, and "immense crowds applied for admittance." For the most part, however, high society held nervously aloof. "The best people," who a few years earlier had chased after him and boasted of his acquaintance, feared contact with the returning exile even when he was dead. True, when the hearse left London on the long drive to Nottinghamshire, it was escorted for the first mile or two by a procession of nearly fifty carriages—Hobhouse and other loyal friends had seen to that—but most of the carriages were empty, sent as a conventional sign of respect but no more. Their aristocratic owners stayed away.

It was different when the coffin reached Nottingham four days later. Again it lay in state in the town's principal inn, the Blackamoor's Head, and the public were admitted in parties of twenty to file respectfully through the parlor. The bells of the parish church tolled, the Town Clerk presented a resolution passed by the Council, and special constables were on duty to control the crowds. Next day, for the final stage of the journey to the church at Hucknall Torkard, near Newstead, the procession of mourners stretched for a quarter of a mile.

The Byrons might no longer own an acre of Newstead, but the family vault was still theirs in the chancel of the little village church. So the poet was placed with his ancestors, in the last remaining corner of his inheritance.

Today, Newstead is really Byron's again, for in 1931 it was bought by a wealthy benefactor and presented to the citizens of Nottingham as a museum of relics connected with him. On that occasion the Prime Minister of Greece made the long journey to pay tribute to his memory. For though Byron never had the chance to fire a shot against the Turks, he had made a contribution to the Greek cause that has never been forgotten. The Greeks had some bitter setbacks after his death and Missolonghi itself fell to the Turks, who set up a ghastly display of three thousand heads. But other British volunteers followed in Byron's footsteps. One, Lord Cochrane, was made commander of the Greek fleet, and another, General Church, became leader of their land forces. Finally, in 1827, the combined warships of Britain, France, and Russia intervened to destroy the Turkish navy at Navarino, and the independence of Greece was established. The public opinion of Europe had made this possible, and in forming that opinion Byron's example had done a great deal.

So ended that chapter of the Greek story. And what, it is natural to wonder, happened to the other characters in Byron's own story?

Two of his early loves did not live long after him. Caroline Lamb died in 1828: her unbalanced, overemotional nature seems to have been seriously affected by his death. Mary Chaworth's end was similarly hastened by shock when the 1831 Reform rioters attacked her home outside Nottingham, before marching off to burn the castle.

"Dearest Augusta" lived on till 1851. Byron's daughter, Ada, survived only a year longer. She had grown up to marry Lord Lovelace, but she died in 1852, at thirty-six, the same age as the father she had never known, and was united with him at last in the family tomb at Hucknall Torkard.

Her mother lived for another eight years. She had become friendly with Harriet Beecher Stowe, author of *Uncle Tom's Cabin,* and after her death that lady wrote a very one-sided book entitled *Lady Byron Vindicated: A History of the Byron Controversy*. Hobhouse, on the other hand, defended Byron's memory with the utmost loyalty throughout his long life. He died in 1869, a prominent figure in British politics.

Teresa Guiccioli never forgot her lover. For a short time she went back to her husband, only to leave him again. She had superficial affairs with various men, including the French poet, Lamartine. When the old Count died at last in 1840, leaving her free to marry again, she waited until 1851 before accepting the most patient of her suitors, the Marquis de Boissy. But she never concealed her devotion to Byron's memory, and gloried sentimentally in the association. Even the Marquis boasted that his wife had once been Byron's mistress. In 1868 she published her own romantic recollections of the affair. She died in 1873.

Claire was the last survivor of those who had known Byron only too well. She had a long and checkered career. She worked as a governess in Russia and Italy, and lived also in Paris and Vienna. The rascally Trelawny wooed her at one time—he had deserted a wife in England—but she would not have him. She became a Roman Catholic, and her last days were spent in Florence, where she died in 1879.

Innumerable books were written by those who had been acquainted with Byron, whether intimately like Teresa or briefly and superficially like Lady Blessington. Though all firsthand impressions, such books often seem to contradict one another and increase the difficulty of discovering the truth. One book that might have solved some enigmas is unfortunately lost forever.

This was Byron's own version, a manuscript he handed to Tom Moore at La Mira in 1819, calling it "My Life and Adventures" and insisting that it must not be published while he lived. No one knows what was in this autobiography, written soon after his settling in Venice. The manuscript was lodged with John Murray and read by various people when the news of Byron's death reached England. Murray and Hobhouse felt it was too frank and should be burned. Representatives of Annabella and Augusta attended a conference in the publisher's drawing room, and these gentlemen also demanded that the memoirs should not be published. Moore was outvoted. Murray compensated him for the money he would lose by the decision, and the unique manuscript was there and then destroyed in the grate. The curled ashen flakes of paper went whirling up the publisher's chimney, and with them went Byron's own explanation.

Now, for most people, the loose ends and unsolved questions seem less important than the indisputable facts of Byron's life and work. These lesser men and women are forgotten, or remembered solely because of their connection with him. Only Byron himself really lives on and matters to us.

He lives in his poetry and his letters. He lives also in spirit in the rooms and gardens of Newstead Abbey, for those who are able to go there on their own Childe Harold's Pilgrimage.

His bedroom can be seen with the curtains he brought from Cambridge. Boatswain's tomb lies outside the windows, Boatswain's collar is preserved indoors. There are letters from Augusta, and Fletcher's letter to her from Greece, breaking the news of Byron's death, and a section of tree trunk from Devil's Wood, on the estate, where Byron carved Augusta's name and his own during their visit in 1814. There are his lordship's boxing gloves and fencing foils, and the sword and plumed helmet he took to Missolonghi. And, perhaps most significant and poignant of all the hundreds of exhibits—books, manuscripts, portraits, and personal possessions—is the pair of wooden shoe lasts, made for a limping boy at the outset of his tragic journey into the adult world.

Chronology of Byron's Life and Times

1788 Byron born in London on January 22.
1789 French Revolution begins.
1798 Byron inherits title. Wordsworth and Coleridge publish *Lyrical Ballads*.
1799 Death of George Washington.
1801 Byron goes to Harrow School.
1805 Byron enters Cambridge. Nelson killed at Trafalgar.
1808 Beethoven's Fifth and Sixth symphonies written.
1809 Byron publishes *English Bards and Scotch Reviewers,* and goes abroad to tour southern Europe until 1811.
1812 *Childe Harold's Pilgrimage* finished. Napoleon's retreat from Moscow. United States at war with Great Britain.
1813 Jane Austen's *Pride and Prejudice* published.
1815 Byron marries Annabella Milbanke. Battle of Waterloo.
1816 Marriage breaks up. Byron goes to Switzerland, and

on to Italy, where he lives in various places—Venice, Ravenna, Pisa, and Genoa—until 1823.

1818   *Don Juan,* first part, published.

1820   Death of King George III. Scott publishes *Ivanhoe.*

1821   Keats dies in Rome.

1822   Shelley drowns at sea. Schubert's "Unfinished" Symphony written.

1823   Byron leaves Italy for Greece.

1824   Byron dies at Missolonghi on April 19.

Some Books for Further Reading

Byron's own poems and letters in various editions.

Buxton, John. *Byron and Shelley: The History of a Friendship*. London: Macmillan, 1968.

Elwin, Malcolm. *Lord Byron's Wife*. New York: Harcourt, Brace & World, 1963.

Marchand, Leslie A. *Lord Byron, A Biography*. New York: Alfred A. Knopf, 1957. (The longest, fullest, and best for quick reference to all the documented facts.)

Maurois, Andre. *Ariel*. New York: Appleton-Century-Crofts, 1924.

———. *Byron*. New York: Appleton-Century-Crofts, 1930.

Nicolson, Harold G. *Byron, The Last Journey*. Boston: Houghton Mifflin, 1924.

Origo, Iris. *The Last Attachment*. New York: Charles Scribner's Sons, 1949.

Quennell, Peter. *Byron, The Years of Fame*. Hamden, Conn.: Shoestring Press, 1967.

———. *Byron in Italy*. New York: The Viking Press, 1957.

Index

About the Author

Born in Nottingham, England, Geoffrey Trease attended
Queen's College Oxford, and has traveled widely in Europe
including most of the places Byron visited in Portugal, Spain,
Italy, Greece and Switzerland. He published his first book
when he was twenty-four and in 1966 won the *New York Her-
ald Tribune* Award when *This is Your Country* was chosen
the best book published in the U.S.A. for the twelve-to-sixteen
age group. A distinguished English author, known for his skill
in writing historical fiction and biographies, Mr. Trease now
resides with his wife in the idyllic English countryside of
Herefordshire.